To my wife, and better two-thirds, Megan.

Contents

Acknowledgments

First and foremost, I would like to thank the Lord for His goodness to me and my family. I also want to especially thank my wife for her encouragement and help. I thank my family members and friends who have encouraged me in pursuing an education and career in religious studies.

I want to acknowledge the following people:

Stephen M. R. Covey, who, despite his exhaustive schedule of traveling the world giving seminars, reserved time to read and endorse the manuscript.

To Robert L. Millet for reading the manuscript and offering many suggestions and advice.

To Paula Hicken for her meticulous review and phenomenal editing service.

To the several staff and students at BYU for their work on source checking: Jessica Hicks, Katie Cannon, Miguel Frias Garcia, Hunter Giles, Lindsay Kekoolani, Hayoung Lee, Luke Oscarson, David Steed, Addie Wallace, Matthew Wilkinson, Jackie Wray.

To McKell Parsons at Cedar Fort for working with me every step of the way and for offering advice on ways to improve parts of the book.

To Shawnda and Deborah and the rest of the Cedar Fort staff for their work and enthusiasm for this book.

Finally, I want to thank all those who purchased this book for their love of studying the gospel and for seeking more knowledge.

Introduction

Roughly two hundred years ago, one particular individual experienced something remarkable—a life changing event—that he would later publish to the world. This occurred during a time of deep reflection and intense depression of the soul. As he lay struggling with darkness, he saw a vision filled with light that grew brighter and brighter. He saw two personages, each in the form of a man. He was filled with love and joy as they told him of a greater work that would soon be manifest by an angel flying in the midst of heaven who would restore the everlasting gospel. This man, Norris Stearns of Greenfield, Massachusetts, was one of many who recorded visionary experiences just before and during Joseph Smith's generation.

As the Lord prepared the earth for the Restoration, numerous individuals recorded experiences of spiritual manifestations. Readers will find that these experiences influenced the process of the Restoration of Christ's Church, even though many of these individuals had never met Joseph Smith or heard of his manifestations at the time they recorded their own. Latter-day Saints are familiar with some of the accounts presented in this book; however, several accounts are not widely known. Many times, these spiritual manifestations prepared and led individuals to the restored gospel.

Meanwhile, Joseph Smith was being called to bring about the Restoration of God's Church on the earth. The appearance of God the Father and Jesus Christ to Joseph Smith was the first of hundreds of manifestations he experienced. Many of these manifestations assisted the Prophet Joseph in restoring Christ's Church to the earth. This period in Church history is characterized by a flood of visions, dreams, revelations, and other episodes of divine instruction.

This book is the result of many years of researching and gathering accounts from articles, biographies, books, and journals relating to the Restoration of Christ's Church. Readers will find hundreds of statements and accounts from Joseph Smith, his fellow Saints, and non-Mormons who claimed to have experienced miraculous events, or who claimed to have seen beyond the veil in the eighteenth and nineteenth centuries. These accounts are defining experiences in the lives of these individuals, as well as in Latter-day Saint history.

The purpose of this book is twofold: (1) to retell the story of the Restoration while highlighting significant events, accounts, and facts that are often overlooked, and (2) to illustrate that the Restoration was a process that developed within a culture that was divinely prepared (for example, visions, manifestations, and spiritual gifts were not new to people living in this "restoration" culture).

The present volume was written with the average Latter-day Saint reader in mind. Although much of my research in religious studies is academic, I wrote this book in a more popular (semi-academic) style. Scholars have been researching some of these issues for two or three decades, but many Latter-day Saints are unaware of them because they are presented in scholarly articles and books. This book is an attempt to present a combination of scholarly information and firsthand accounts about Joseph Smith's experiences and the early days of the Church in an accessible and faith-promoting manner.

This book has been organized and divided into six chapters.

Chapter 1 discusses Joseph Smith's First Vision in relation to visions that his Christian contemporaries recorded. These individuals lived in the Northeast region and recorded their experiences between 1740 and 1830. This is significant in understanding the culture in which Father Smith, Mother Smith, Joseph, and his siblings were raised. Many people not only claimed to have seen visions during these few generations, but many claimed to have seen God the Father and Jesus Christ. These accounts show, among other things, that Joseph Smith was not the only person who claimed to see visions, that the heavens were not sealed as many Christians claim, and that God began enlightening the minds of individuals in preparation for the Restoration prior to Joseph's First Vision. Moreover, these accounts offer additional testimony regarding the nature of God, the existence of angels, and the reality of Satan.

Chapter 2 also deals with one aspect of the First Vision: namely, the commandment given to Joseph not to join any church because they were all corrupt. The first portion of this chapter is a brief commentary on that commandment. The next section includes statements from Christians of past centuries who also believed that an apostasy from Christ's Church occurred and that a restoration was necessary. The last section contains accounts from individuals who saw visions (shortly before the organization of the Church in 1830) informing them that Christ's Church had become corrupt and that it would be restored in the near future.

Chapter 3 discusses the role that ancient prophets played in the Restoration. The first half of this chapter discusses Moroni's appearances to Joseph Smith between September 1823 and June 1829 and also the ancient connections and prophetic significance of these visits. The second half of the chapter describes other ancient prophets who appeared to Joseph and others in the early days of the Restoration to assist in the translation of the gold plates and Bible, to command certain actions to be performed, or to restore various keys to the earth.

Chapter 4 contains accounts from several early Saints whom

the Lord permitted to either see or handle the plates. They describe its weight and size, the characters inscribed on them, and the background of why the Lord permitted them to see or touch the plates. The concluding pages of the chapter contain descriptions of other ancient metallic plates that were discovered within the past fifty years. Certain characteristics of these metallic records provide additional insight into the gold plates and its appearance.

Chapter 5 explains the role of the Urim and Thummim and seer stones in the Restoration. The Urim and Thummim was used for more than just translating the plates. Joseph also used it to receive revelations. In addition, the Lord permitted Joseph to use a seer stone in translating portions of the plates as well as the Bible. Moreover, the Prophet Joseph saw the entire history of the Bible, his own history, and the history of several other men in a seer stone and the Urim and Thummim.

Chapter 6 contains several accounts of early Saints who saw visions or witnessed some kind of manifestation that led them to the Church. Some were told in visions or dreams to seek out the Saints and be baptized, some witnessed miraculous healings that influenced them into joining the Church, and others saw visions shortly after their baptisms confirming that their decision to join the Church was right.

Chapter One

Joseph Smith's First Vision and a Culture of Spiritual Manifestations

The purpose of this chapter is not to recount and analyze Joseph Smith's First Vision, as others have already attempted that several times. Rather, it is to juxtapose the First Vision with accounts of other visionaries in the eighteenth and nineteenth centuries and to discuss the religious atmosphere in which these visionaries lived.

In the decades following the Revolutionary War, Americans witnessed arguably the most intense religious revival in American history—the Second Great Awakening. Historians date this religious awakening from approximately 1800 to 1830. This period in American religious history was paramount for several reasons. The country was still reeling from the Revolutionary War and the War of 1812. Families were recovering from the loss of loved ones, men were struggling to earn money to support their families, and the religiosity of average Americans was low compared to other generations. Unlike the First Great Awakening of the 1730s and 1740s, when religious sermons were aimed at churchgoers, the preachers of the Second Great Awakening directed their sermons to nonchurchgoers. Well-known preachers like Charles G. Finney, Lorenzo Dow, and Peter Cartwright traveled throughout the states preaching, converting, and baptizing.

Teachers of all religious groups held street meetings that

often lasted the entire day and extended into the night. These meetings were sometimes called *revivals*. Joseph Smith Jr. remembered that the revivals "commenced with the Methodists, but soon became general among all the sects in that region of country." "Indeed," continued Smith, "the whole district of the country seemed affected by it and great multitudes united themselves to the different religious parties. . . . Some were contending for the Methodist faith, some for the Presbyterian, and some for the Baptist." As people began to join their desired religious sect, "great confusion and bad feeling ensued; priest contending against priest, and convert against convert; so that all their good feelings one for another, if they ever had any, were entirely lost in a strife of words and a contest about opinions."[1] As a result of these revivals, people began joining religious sects and attending their meetings.

The events of the Second Great Awakening resulted in the founding of many religions and organizations interested in temperance, slavery abolition, and women's rights. Individuals and families of this generation felt free to worship as they pleased, and any person, regardless of his or her level of education, felt capable of interpreting scripture and teaching fellow Christians. Had this not been the case, Joseph Smith Jr.—an ordinary farmer—would not have been successful in gaining followers. As the well-known historian Gordon Wood observed, Mormonism began at the perfect time. Had someone attempted to found a religion like Mormonism a few generations earlier or later than 1830, it probably would have failed miserably.[2]

The trend of attending religious street meetings and investigating preachers and churches was accompanied by discussions and sermons of revelations, heavenly manifestations, and spiritual gifts. In 1830, Jewish religious zealot Robert Matthews claimed to have received a revelation wherein God appointed him to be a prophet. He subsequently traveled the States and preached the imminent arrival of the millennium, which was common.[3] Preachers and missionaries captivated audiences and stirred emotions by recounting manifestations and other spiritual gifts that had affected people in their congregations.

The religious culture of both the First and Second Great Awakenings also produced numerous visionaries who published their manifestations in newspapers and pamphlets. Reverend Nicholas Gilman of Durham, New Hampshire, stated in 1742 that visions and heavenly experiences were main topics of conversation among the religious populace, not just professional clergy and theologians.[4] Douglas Winiarski observed that "Methodists, Baptists, and radical sectarians would load their diaries, memoirs, autobiographies, and published writings with numerous references to audible voices, visions, and various kinds of supernatural visitations."[5] Susan Juster, a non-LDS scholar, identified over three hundred individuals who claimed visionary experiences during the generation of Joseph Smith's parents.[6] Congregationalist minister Charles Chauncy of Boston stated that claims of seeing visions were common.[7]

A few years after Joseph Smith's First Vision, near the end of the Second Great Awakening, Mormon missionaries were among those who found success in gaining converts. Many of these converts had already accepted the idea of a restoration and had sought for a church that possessed the spiritual gifts common among first-century Christians. Mormon missionaries, similar to other preachers during this era, held street meetings where dozens and sometimes hundreds of people would gather to listen. They preached at length about prophets, apostles, visions, and other spiritual gifts that accompanied the young Church. They often quoted religious figures like Martin Luther and John Wesley, who discussed the significance of spiritual gifts in the latter days. John G. Whittier, a member of the Shaker movement, described Mormon claims of possessing spiritual gifts as follows:

> They contrast strongly the miraculous power of the gospel in the apostolic time with the present state of our nominal Christianity. They ask for the signs of divine power; the faith, overcoming all

> things, which opened the prison doors of the apostles, gave them power over the elements, which rebuked disease and death itself, and made visible to all the presence of the living God. They ask for any declaration in the Scriptures that this miraculous power of faith was to be confined to the first confessors of Christianity. They speak a language of hope and promise to weak, weary hearts, tossed and troubled, who have wandered from sect to sect, seeking in vain for the primal manifestations of the divine power.[8]

The religious culture of the First and Second Great Awakening prepared thousands for the Restoration of the Church. Spiritual gifts, visions, dreams, and other heavenly manifestations were common. It is not surprising, then, to learn that Joseph Smith's parents believed him when he recounted visions and manifestations he had witnessed. After conversing with Joseph Smith on three separate occasions during the night of September 21, 1823, and again the next morning, the angel Moroni commanded Joseph to relate what he had seen and heard to his father. "I returned back to my father in the field," recalled Joseph, "and rehearsed the whole matter to him. He replied to me, that it was of God, and to go and do as commanded by the messenger."[9] Joseph's father, a skeptic regarding organized Protestant religion, would have been aware of the visionary accounts that had circulated throughout the region. Indeed, Joseph Smith Sr. was a visionary man himself. His wife, Lucy, recorded at least seven of his heavenly manifestations years prior to their son's First Vision in 1820 (see chapter 2).[10]

Joseph Smith's First Vision

Below are accounts of twenty individuals (including Joseph Smith Jr.) who recorded divine manifestations of a similar nature. All twenty visions presented here occurred in the northeastern states region and were recorded sometime between the First Great Awakening and Second Great Awakening (1740s–1830s). The accounts following the discussion of Joseph's First Vision are presented in chronological order.

Joseph Smith Jr., like scores of his contemporaries, was consumed with finding answers to various questions concerning religion and salvation. "Who of all these parties are right?" Joseph asked himself, "Or are they all wrong together? And if any one of them be right which is it? And how shall I know it?"[11] Joseph answered his own questions when he wrote, "Considering that all could not be right and that God could not be the author of so much confusion, I determined to investigate the subject more fully, believing that if God had a Church it would not be split up into factions, and that if He taught one society to worship one way, and administer in one set of ordinances, He would not teach another principles which were diametrically opposed."[12]

One day while reading the Bible (an unusual activity for a teenage boy), he discovered a passage in the Epistle of James (1:5): "If any of you lack wisdom, let him ask of God." Joseph recalled that the message entered his "heart" with "more power" than he ever felt before. He "reflected on it again and again" until it consumed his every thought.[13] His mother remembered that Joseph "had never read the Bible through in his life: he seemed much less inclined to the perusal of books than any of the rest of our children."[14] If so, who persuaded the young teenager to open the Bible and read it? William Smith, Joseph's younger brother, explained:

> There was a joint revival in the neighborhood between the Baptists, Methodists and Presbyterians and they had succeeded in stirring up quite a feeling, and after the meeting the question arose which church should have the converts. Rev. Stockton was the president of the meeting and suggested it was their meeting and under their care and they had a church there and they ought to join the Presbyterians, but as father did not like Rev. Stockton very well, our folks hesitated and the next evening a Rev. Mr. Lane of the Methodists preached a sermon on 'what church shall I join?' And the burden of the discourse was to ask God, using as a text, 'If any man lack wisdom let him ask of God who giveth to all men liberally.' And of course when Joseph went home and was looking over the text he was impressed to do just what the preacher had said.[15]

Joseph later explained that he secluded himself to pray on the Smith family property "in the woods where my father had a clearing" and at the "stump where I had stuck my axe when I had quit work." Joseph began his prayer, "O Lord, what Church shall I join?"[16]

Orson Hyde reported that Joseph told him that while praying "the adversary . . . filled his mind with doubts and brought to mind all manner of inappropriate images to prevent him from obtaining" answers to his questions.[17] Another account claimed that Joseph's tongue swelled in his mouth so that he could not speak. He also explained, "I heard a noise behind me like someone walking towards me. . . . the noise of walking seemed to draw nearer, I sprang upon my feet and looked round, but saw no person, or thing that was calculated to produce the noise of walking."[18] He was seized subsequently upon by an "unseen" force and "thick darkness" gathered around him. Just as he thought he would "sink into despair and . . . destruction," he saw a vision.[19] "A pillar of fire light above the brightness of the sun at noon day came down from above and rested upon me and I was filled with the Spirit of God and the Lord opened the heavens upon me and I saw the Lord"[20] who appeared in the midst of a "pillar of flame, which was spread all around and yet nothing consumed." Soon after, another personage appeared who exactly resembled the other "in features, and likeness."[21] He learned that these two heavenly beings were God the Father and Jesus Christ. The most well known account of this manifestation relates succinctly to what Joseph experienced.

> I saw a pillar of light exactly over my head above the brightness of the sun, which descended gradually until it fell upon me. It no sooner appeared than I found myself delivered from the enemy which held me bound. When the light rested upon me I saw two personages (whose brightness and glory defy all description) standing above me in the air. One of them spake unto me calling me by name and said (pointing to the other) "This is my beloved Son, Hear him. . . ."

> I asked the personages who stood above me in the light, which of all the sects was right, (for at this time it had never entered into my heart that all were wrong) and which I should join. I was answered that I must join none of them, for they were all wrong, and the Personage who addressed me said that all their Creeds were an abomination in his sight, that those professors were all corrupt, that "they draw near to me with their lips but their hearts are far from me, They teach for doctrines the commandments of men, having a form of Godliness but they deny the power thereof."[22]

Note the following details of Joseph's First Vision while reading accounts of Joseph's contemporaries below: (1) Joseph saw two personages each in the form of a man, (2) Christ literally stood at the Father's right-hand side as a separate and distinct being, (3) the Father and Christ looked alike, (4) the surroundings appeared to be on fire, and (5) an evil influence was present shortly before the vision.

Joseph Smith's Contemporaries

Reverend Benjamin Pomeroy

In 1741, Benjamin Pomeroy, minister of the Congregational Church in Hebron, Connecticut, recorded in his diary a vision that a member of his congregation saw while attending a church service. The vision came to the individual while pondering a sermon on Isaiah chapter 40. Pomeroy recorded that the individual fainted and then awoke to find himself at the foot of a mountain. A heavenly personage appeared and escorted the visionary to the gates of heaven where God and Christ were seen sitting on their thrones in all their glory. He also saw "angels bowing and paying their homage and adoration to them." At this incredible sight he felt out of place. Sensing his insecurity, Christ approached and showed him his "name written in Letters of blood." Christ then smiled and commanded him to return to his body where he would be blessed to "withstand all temptation." Instantly, another vision came and the individual saw "the mouth of hell open." He saw Satan standing before him and was told that "he would have me." The vision closed shortly thereafter and the individual found his "body all disordered with the Cramp."[23]

This vision was similar to Joseph Smith's First Vision in that the man saw two separate individuals—God the Father and Jesus the Christ. He also experienced the presence of Satan who tried to discourage him, much like Joseph Smith.

Isaiah Pratt

In 1741, just two weeks after the previous vision occurred, the first minister of the Congregational Church in Westborough, Massachusetts, Reverend Ebenezer Parkman, witnessed a member of his congregation enter into a trance. This individual, Isaiah Pratt, remained in that state for more than twenty-four hours. When Pratt came out of the trance, he claimed that he had "seen hell, and seen Christ." Reverend Parkman related more of what Pratt saw:

> He . . . informed me of his seeing (as he thought) the devil, who met him as he seemed to be in the way towards heaven, and told him that there was no room for him there; of his seeing hell, and hearing the most dreadful noise of roaring and crying; his seeing heaven, so wondrously happy a place as nobody could tell but those that were there; and Christ, who looked more pleasant than ever he had seen any man, and who had a great book before him, and in turning over the leaves of it, told him that his name was there, and showed it [to] him; and that he had seen a great many more things, which were such great things that he could not speak of them.[24]

Pratt described Christ, in heaven, as a "man" and not as a mystic being without body, parts, or passions. Pratt, like the previous visionary, saw Satan, who tried to discourage him, saying that there was no room for him in heaven. Speaking of this very theme, Brigham Young taught, "When individuals are blessed with visions, revelations, and great manifestations, look out, then the devil is nigh you, and you will be tempted in proportion to the vision, revelation, or manifestation you have received."[25]

Reverend Daniel Rogers

In 1740–41 Daniel Rogers, the well-known Unitarian minister of Ipswich, Massachusetts, conducted a preaching tour throughout the New England states. During the tour he encountered many people who claimed to have seen visions. He encountered others who were "Transported to Heaven" who saw the "Glories of Christ." He was particularly impressed with the vision of one "*young lad*" whose "spirit had been drawn out & carried up to Heaven where He had a View" of Jesus Christ "in *Glory sitting at the right Hand of God*." He also saw surrounding angels, which included his deceased grandfather.[26]

Joseph Bean

Joseph Bean of Cambridge, Massachusetts, set aside one hour per night for prayer and meditation. On one particular night in 1741, he was caught up in a vision where he saw the "immaculate lamb of God hanging upon the Cursed tree . . . with his arms widely Extended." A few months later in the spring of 1742, he beheld another vision. He described seeing "God and *Christ at his right hand* and the burning throne with millions of shining angels in postures of adoration." Bean also claimed to have seen his "name in the records of heaven the lamb's book of life."[27]

Joseph Smith, like Joseph Bean, saw Christ standing at the right hand of God, as well as a multitude of angelic beings. Bean described them as appearing to be "burning" and "shining." Joseph Smith described the angelic personages as an "eclipse" at "noon-day" and that he expected the trees to be consumed with fire.

Benjamin Abbott

In 1772 Benjamin Abbott, a Methodist minister of Pittsgrove Township, New Jersey, was torn between joining with the Baptists and Presbyterians. During this time, he recorded several visions of evil spirits as well as of Christ on at least two occasions. During this process of deciding which church to join, Abbott battled feelings of despair and unworthiness that led to many horrific dreams and visions of Satan. One night he dreamt he was transported to hell and tortured by evil spirits. This frightened him immensely and caused him to become more active in prayer. Five weeks later he dreamt that he was taken to heaven where he saw "elegant buildings" and an assembly of personages dressed in "white raiment," which hung to their feet. He also saw God "sitting upon his throne." Despite this dream, Abbott continued to struggle with anxiety and depression. He related a life-changing experience that occurred a short while later.

> One day going to the mill, I felt such a hell in my breast arising from a guilty conscience . . . and I was passing through a piece of woods, the devil suddenly suggested to my mind, that as I was one of the reprobates and there was no mercy for me, I had better hang myself and know the worst of it. While I was looking for a suitable place for that purpose, I thought I heard a voice saying "This torment is nothing to hell." I immediately changed my mind and drove home under the greatest anxiety imaginable, for it appeared to me the devil was behind me in the wagon with his hands just over my head, threatening to take me away both soul and body. I cannot express any feelings at that time, my hair arose on my head through fear. I was afraid to look back, lest I should visibly see him. In this deplorable condition I returned home; when I got into the house I dared not go outside of the door, for fear the devil would take me away. My wife saw that something was the matter with me and enquired what it was, for, said she, "you look like death." I was constrained to turn from her and weep, for I expected she knew my condition, as she had been a member of the Presbyterian Church for many years, and was a praying woman.

Two nights later, Abbott saw a remarkable vision.

> That night I lay alone, expecting to sleep little, but to pray and weep all night; whenever I fell into a slumber, it appeared to me that I saw hell opened ready to receive me, and I just on

> the point of dropping in, and devils waiting to seize me. Being thus alarmed, it would arouse me up, crying to the Lord to save me—and thus I passed the whole night in this terrified unhappy condition. Just at the dawning of the day, I fell into a doze more like sleep than any I had during the whole night, in which I dreamed that I saw a river as clear as chrystal [*sic*] . . . I immediately hastened to the river, and went in, the water running over my head . . . at that instant I awoke, and saw, by faith, the Lord Jesus Christ standing by me, with his arms extended wide, saying to me, "I died for you." I *then looked up, and by faith I saw the Ancient of Days*. . . . Then by faith I saw the Lord Jesus come to me as with a cup in his hand, and he gave it to me, and I took it and drank thereof. . . . The river which I saw, represented to me the river of life proceeding from the throne of God.

Following these experiences, Abbott joined the Methodists, as he found their teachings to be the most correct of all the Christian churches.[28]

Benjamin Abbott and Joseph Smith both experienced the torment of Satan before seeing God and Christ. This state of demonic torture caused them to call upon God to save them. Abbott, like Joseph Smith, saw God and Christ as two separate personages. Note that Doctrine and Covenants 27:11 designates Adam as the "Ancient of Days;" however, other Christian commentators in previous generations associated God the Father with that title.

Thomas Rankin

In 1773, John Wesley sent Thomas Rankin of Dunbar, Scotland, to America to lead the Methodist Church in New England. For reasons unknown, Rankin experienced depression after his arrival, which became so great that he wished to die. One night while in Philadelphia, a vision opened to him in which he saw evil spirits. "Some may think or suppose [it] was only a dream," stated Rankin, "but of the contrary of this, I am assured of, as I know I am at this moment a living man. . . . [I] clearly saw, my soul doomed to everlasting flames. . . . Around my bed, stood with eager looks, a company of damned spirits, ready to conduct my soul to endless torments." After he saw these evil spirits, he beheld another vision. "In the twinkling of an eye, I beheld the heavens open and part asunder and the appearance of the glorified humanity of the Son of God. I thought I cried aloud, 'There is the Lord Jesus Christ! There is the Redeemer of lost and undone mankind!'" The next time he preached at a major gathering, he related that "it seemed as if the very house shook with the mighty power and glory of Sinai's God. . . . As for myself, I scarce knew whether I was in the body or not; and so it was with all my brethren."[29]

Lorenzo Dow

Lorenzo Dow

In the late 1770s, a twelve-year-old boy living in Coventry, Connecticut, claimed to have seen visions. This boy, Lorenzo Dow, later became a key figure in the Second Great Awakening and a well-known minister of the Methodist Church. During his ministry other Methodist leaders became displeased with him because he preached to everyone, not just Methodists. At the age of twelve, he claimed to have seen a vision of the biblical prophet Nathan, who ministered during the reign of King David. The next year, at age thirteen, he was shown a vision of heaven in which he saw "God, Jesus and the angel Gabriel."[30]

Dow's experience is significant because of his age. He was thirteen years old when he saw both God and Jesus. Joseph Smith was fourteen when he saw God the Father and Jesus for the first time. Joseph Smith, Lorenzo Dow, and others mentioned in this chapter were a few of many teenagers who saw visions during this generation. Robert Remini, a non-LDS historian noted that "During the Second Great Awakening many . . . adolescents claimed to have seen and talked with God the Father and His Son, Jesus Christ."[31]

Caleb Rich

One day in 1778, Caleb Rich, a Baptist from Warwick, Massachusetts, felt "as it were a shock of electricity, my lips quivered, my flesh trembled, and felt a tremour throughout my whole frame." Rich looked up and saw "Jesus the Christ of God" as "a beautiful personage" of "an unspeakable grace, mercy, meekness, mildness, loving kindness, gentleness, and compassion." Christ gave him "two small portions of food resembling corn" and said, "Eat sufficiently of it thyself; and of it feed my sheep and lambs, and it will never exhaust, it will be sufficient for thee at all times."[32] Rich saw another vision of an angel, who told him not to join any existing churches, as they were without "apostolic rectitude" (see chapter 2).

Elias Smith

Elias Smith

In the 1790s, Baptist minister Elias Smith of Lyme, Connecticut, felt guilty as a result of sin and was extremely depressed over questions concerning religion and salvation. One day while gathering wood, Smith slipped and fell on his back. With his leg trapped under a log he looked into the sky and saw the following:

> A light appeared to shine from heaven, not only into my head, but into my heart. . . . My mind seemed to rise in that light to the throne of God and the Lamb, and while thus gloriously led, what appeared to my understanding was expressed in Rev. 14:1: "and I looked, and, lo, a Lamb stood on the mount Sion, and with him an hundred forty and four thousand, having his father's name

> written in their foreheads." The Lamb once slain appeared to my understanding, and while viewing him, I felt such love to him as I never felt to any thing earthly. My mind was calm and at peace with God through the Lamb of God, that taketh away the sin of the world. The view of the Lamb on mount Sion gave me joy unspeakable and full of glory.[33]

Nathan Culver

Nathan Culver was born into a religious family who eventually helped establish the first Baptist Church in Groton, Connecticut. Culver, believing that neither heaven nor hell existed, began to resent the Bible because of people constantly preaching at him. Culver described himself as being "on the brink of ruin." In 1791, Culver recorded seeing the following vision:

> I went to bed as usual, but slept none 'till late, for trouble of mind. . . . I was risen up in the bed, and was praying to God that if there was any Heaven or Hell I might instantly know it. . . . The same instant I saw a man in the room with a bright shining light around him, which *appeared brighter than the sun*, shining in his full strength . . . and bid me fear not and follow him. . . . I was carried to the most glorious city, which shone with such brightness that it dazzled my eyes to behold it. Then I was brought to the bar of God's awful justice, and *Christ took his seat on the right-hand* of power. . . . It appeared to me that the awful Judge opened a very great book, which contained the names of the righteous and the wicked. . . . Then I heard the . . . Judge pronounce his glorious name Jehovah which caused the Heavens to rejoice and Hell to tremble; and he likewise said, if ever I made game of that *Holy Name*, I should never have a right there, and the gates should be forever shut against me. . . . It appeared to me that the Judge held over my head a great sword of justice, ready to take vengeance on me. But in the midst of my fears . . . Jesus Christ came and kneeled down between me and the bar of God, and like a *Mediator* plead my cause in a mist affecting manner, and said, "O *Father*, I have died for this sinner! And now, O *Father*, spare this sinner! O *Father*, I stand between him and the stroke of thy wrath! O *Father*, why should he die?" And at these words of the Mediator, the justice of God seemed to be silent; and God was well pleased with what Christ had said on my behalf, and Christ

> turned to me with a smiling face, and said, "Your sins are forgiven, and your transgressions I will remember no more." Then he shewed me, and bid me look and see the prints of the nails in his hands; "this," said he, "I bore for you."[34]

Nathan Culver, like Joseph Smith, recorded that his room gradually got brighter until it was "brighter than the sun" and that Christ sat at his father's right-hand side. Perhaps the most important aspect of this account is that it teaches and expounds on a key doctrine—justice and mercy. It also provides a magnificent explanation of two of Christ's eternal roles, namely, Judge and Mediator.

Sarah Alley

In February 1798, Sarah Alley of Beekman Town, New York, claimed to have been taken to heaven in vision. After falling from a chair, Alley lay lifeless for several hours. While unconscious, she beheld a vision of heaven.

> I left the body, and found a guide ready to take charge of and conduct me, which I knew to be an angel, and who continued with me during the vision. He first took me to the borders of that lake and pit where there is continual weeping and lamentation. I went so near the side and borders of it that it seemed as if I should have fallen therein. . . . I was then conducted by my guide to the place of happiness, where I saw Christ and the holy angels around him, and abundance of people clothed in white robes, but I could not distinguish one from another, so as to know them, being not suffered to enter the kingdom, though I desired the liberty of going in, my guide telling me I must return quickly to the world, for I could not have entrance here. He then conducted me back to my body.[35]

Sarah Alley recorded that she saw Christ in heaven surrounded by holy angels and that she "could not distinguish one from another." Similarly, Joseph Smith recorded that God the Father and Jesus Christ "resembled each other in features and likeness." Later in life, Joseph saw a vision of the Twelve Apostles in which they were ushered into the presence of God and "that they . . . all looked alike."[36] One LDS commentator interpreted this to mean that glorified sons and daughters of God carry similar resemblance like that of a family as well as a similar resemblance in beauty.[37]

Hannah Coy

In September 1798, nine-year-old Hannah Coy of Jericho, Vermont, was taken to heaven in vision. After the vision closed she related to her mother the following details:

> Oh! My dear mama, I have seen him; he is in heaven, and there *I saw Jesus Christ on the right hand of God his Father*, and he is all the time pleading for poor sinners, and shewing his wounded hands and where he was nailed to the cross for poor sinners, and I saw thousands of Saints and angels round the throne, singing glory to God and Jesus Christ. . . . Christ showed me the book of life, and said my name was in it, and that he died to save me and all that would love him. He then took me to the place, mama, that you have told me of so often, which is the world of hell, and there I saw the dreadful distress of multitudes of poor souls in misery . . . there I saw the devil, and a dreadful looking creature he is . . . and he tried with all his might to get hold of me, to pull me into that dreadful place, but Christ prevented him. . . . He then told me to return back, and to tell my father and mother what I had seen, and to tell my father that he must carry me to our minister, and I must tell the minister all that I had seen, and that he must come to my daddy's and preach the gospel.[38]

Nathan Barlow

Like Nathan Culver, Nathan Barlow of Freetown, Maine, doubted whether a place called hell existed and if it was as horrible as his ministers had taught. On January 8, 1801, after attending a religious meeting where the subject of heaven and hell was discussed, Barlow saw a vision.

> About the close of day light I was taken all at once with a strange kind of feeling, and laid me down: I began to grow stiff and to lose the power of moving by degrees . . . I am very clear that I did not fall asleep, nether was I sleepy, it being just dark;

then there came the appearance of a man, with a glorious countenance, who told me he was Christ, and took me by the hand seemingly, and carried me away as quick as a flash of lightning (my spirit I mean, for I was sensible at the time that I had left my body behind, and had no feeling of weight, but light as air.) I was carried to the place of torment, and was hovering over it, and fearful of sinking into it; but Christ told me I should not fall into it. . . . I also saw the Devil in the midst of them; he seemed to be chained there, and in the greatest misery of them all . . . Oh the groans that filled my astonished soul. . . I floated about over this dreadful pit like a feather carried by a small breeze of wind, Christ being with me, and holding me by the hand. . . . I was then carried to the entrance of heaven, but not suffered to enter there: *I saw God*, and the Saints in glory: they looked very smiling, and appeared perfectly happy; their faces were all toward God; and they were singing praises to him in a most melodious manner. . . . Christ gave me a charge to publish what I had seen and heard, in a meeting that was to be in the neighborhood at such a time; and he told me that it would be a fuller meeting than usual, and that most of my relations would be there. I said to this purpose, that I was ignorant and fearful, and could not relate it: He told me to begin, and he would be with me, and put words in my mouth. . . . And now I do, in the most solemn manner, call Almighty God to witness, that I have no design to impose on any one, but have given a true relation of what I have seen and heard, which I certify by signing my name with my own hand. (*Signed*) Nathan Barlow.[39]

Norris Stearns

In 1815, Norris Stearns published, in Greenfield, Massachusetts, a vision he had seen that was similar to the 1820 vision of Joseph Smith. In his vision, which came during a time of inward struggle regarding the meaning in life and religion, Stearns saw God the Father and Jesus Christ. He was told that a "greater work" of God would "soon be made manifest" and that the angel with the "everlasting gospel" would come "to do his work" (for the remainder of the account, not included below, see chapter 2).

> At length, as I lay apparently upon the brink of eternal woe, seeing nothing but death before me, suddenly there came a sweet flow of the love of God to my soul, which gradually increased. At the same time, there appeared a small gleam of light in the room, *above the brightness of the sun*, then at his meridian, which grew brighter and brighter: As this light and love increased, my sins began to separate, and the Mountain removed towards the east. At length, being in an ecstasy of joy, I turned to the other side of the bed, (whether in the body or out I cannot tell, God knoweth) *there I saw two spirits*, which I knew at the first sight. But if I had the tongue of an Angel I could not describe their glory, for they brought the joys of heaven with them. *One was God, my Maker, almost in bodily shape like a man. His face was, as it were a flame of Fire, and his body, as it had been a Pillar and a Cloud.* In looking steadfastly to discern features, I could see none, but a small glimpse would appear in some other place. *Below him stood Jesus Christ my Redeemer, in perfect shape like a man*—His face was not ablaze, but had the countenance of fire, being bright and shining. His Father's will appeared to be his! All was condescension, peace, and love![40]

This account is so similar to Joseph Smith's that it would be difficult to differentiate between them if one was only semifamiliar with Joseph's First Vision accounts. Stearns recorded that he was seized upon by Satan and that he was on "the brink of eternal woe." He explained that the vision "gradually increased" until it appeared "above the brightness of the sun." Stearns also claimed, as did Joseph Smith, Benjamin Abbott, and others, that he saw "two" separate personages "in perfect shape like a man." This is significant because many Protestant churches taught, and continue to teach, that God the Father and Jesus Christ are one entity. Surely Norris Stearns, Joseph Smith, and Benjamin Abbott knew that; therefore, claiming to have seen God and Christ as two separate personages would seem very strange, which strengthens the validity of their claims.

Charles G. Finney

In 1821, Charles G. Finney of Adams, New York, perhaps

Charles G. Finney

"the most prominent revivalist of the day," went into the woods to pray and ask God to forgive his sins. Later that day while sitting in his office, the Savior appeared to him. "*I met the Lord Jesus Christ face to face. . . . I saw him as I would see any other man*," recorded Finney; "it seemed to me a reality that he stood before me, and I fell down at his feet and poured out my soul to him."[41]

Finney, like many other individuals mentioned in this chapter, described seeing the Lord as he would see any "man." His experience was similar to that of Moses as described in Exodus 33:11: "And the Lord spake unto Moses face to face, as a man speaketh unto his friend." Many Christians believe that God does not have a resurrected body but acknowledge that Christ was resurrected and possesses a body of flesh and bones as described in Luke 24:37–39. Following Jesus's resurrection, he appeared to his Apostles. "But they were terrified and affrighted, and supposed that *they had seen a spirit*." Christ, seeing that they were "troubled" said, "Behold my hands and my feet, that it is I myself: handle me, and see; *for a spirit hath not flesh and bones as ye see me have*." Sonce the Bible teaches about Christ's resurrected body of flesh and bones, it seems confusing that some of these Christian groups would teach that Christ and God the Father are one entity.

All the confusion regarding the nature of God is clarified through the Prophet Joseph Smith who saw, in the First Vision, God the Father and Jesus Christ standing before him in the form of two men. The Lord revealed to Joseph Smith in 1843 that "The

Father has a body of flesh and bones as tangible as man's; the Son also" (D&C 130:22). Joseph Smith taught on another occasion, "That which is without body, parts and passions is nothing. There is no other God in heaven but that God who has flesh and bones."[42]

Asa Wild

In 1823, Asa Wild, a Methodist from West Fairlee, Vermont, was told by the Lord in vision that no true church presently existed on the earth and that he was preparing a group of people to restore his Church (see the full account in chapter 2).

Francis G. Bishop

In 1825, sixteen-year-old Francis G. Bishop of Greece, New York, heard sermons of Charles G. Finney (previously mentioned) and became enthused about Christianity. One day while engaged in prayer, a wall with a doorway appeared before him. He saw three personages who walked by the doorway and smiled at him. Suddenly a fourth person appeared who Bishop knew was the "Ancient of Days" of whom he had "read in the Prophecy of Daniel." This visionary experience influenced Bishop immensely throughout his life and in 1832 he came in contact with the Mormons and joined the Church.[43]

Billy Hibbard

In the late 1700s during the Revolutionary War, a young boy named Billy Hibbard had a dream that motivated him to turn to God. In this dream he saw his uncles and his father fighting in the war. Hibbard prayed in his dream that the Lord would keep them safe. Throughout his teenage and young adult years he clung to the scriptures and teachings of Christ. He eventually became a minister for the Methodist Church, and throughout the early years of the 1820s, he resided in Boston and New York. One Sabbath day while reading the Bible, he felt the urge to pray. While walking to a remote spot, Hibbard conjured up feelings of despair and convinced himself that praying for his own needs was selfish. He described his experience as follows:

> I came to the place of prayer, and kneeled down and closed my eyes, *with my hands lifted toward the heavens, I saw Jesus Christ at the right hand of God* looking down upon me, and God the Father looking upon him. The look of Jesus on me removed the burden of my sins, while he spoke these words, "Be faithful unto death and this shall be thy place of rest" . . . the love of God in Christ and of Christ in God, so completely overcame me, that I was all in tears, crying, Glory! Glory! Glory! . . . all nature was praising God. The sun and firmament, the trees, birds, and beasts, all appeared stamped with the glory of God. I leaped from my kneeling posture, clapped my hands, and cried, Glory! Glory! Glory![44]

John Murdock

In 1827, John Murdock, a Campbellite from Kortwright, New York, saw a vision of Jesus Christ that motivated him to search for a church to join. Specifically, he sought for one that possessed the ordinances of salvation.

> One day I was engaged in meditation, and a vision passed before my mind. It appeared to me as if the judgment had sat, and the Lord was on his throne, and called the people to him one at a time and questioned them respecting their conduct in this life; and it appeared as if they answered truly for they durst not answer otherwise; for the judge knew all that was in them, and I thought that I was about the third person called, and the first question put to me was if I had commemorated the death and sufferings of the Savior, by obeying the ordinances, at which I was aroused as from sleep being insensible of the vision, and of my situation, till I found myself convicted of a lack of duty. I immediately began to look for a society that I might receive the ordinances with.[45]

Conclusion

As presented in this chapter and shown in the accompanying chart, the manifestations of these individuals are similar, in some way, to the first visionary experience of Joseph Smith. These accounts teach many truths concerning visions, angels, the nature of God, the nature of Christ, and revelation in modern times. Furthermore, these visions add validity to the Prophet Joseph's claims. They do not imply that Joseph Smith was just another face in the crowd of visionaries. They suggest, rather, that the Lord opened the heavens to the inhabitants of this earth in order to prepare the world, and specifically to prepare a nation, to receive the Restoration.

Also note that not all of these manifestations are equal in scope and meaning; not all of them included all of the elements present in Joseph Smith's vision. These manifestations were granted to various individuals for different purposes. Specifically, the numerous visionaries mentioned in this chapter, as well as in chapter 2, did not claim that their heavenly manifestations had prepared them to oversee the great work in the last days of restoring Christ's Church. While it is true that a few of them attempted to start a religion (for example, Elias Smith and John Noyes; see chapter 2) or claimed to be a prophet (for example, Norris Stearns and Robert Matthews; see above and chapter 2), none of them claimed, like Joseph Smith, that frequent manifestations from heaven prepared them, and gave them authority, to carry out the task of restoring Christ's primitive Church to the earth. These visionaries were informed of the Restoration, were instructed to abandon all Christian sects and search the scriptures, or were charged to share their manifestations with others; however, none of them came close to claiming or accomplishing that which Joseph Smith claimed and accomplished. Further evidence of this is discussed in chapter 2, where it is presented that practitioners of certain restoration churches felt that something was still missing in their religious movement (for example, Sidney Rigdon and Newel and Elizabeth Whitney). Where did they eventually turn? They turned to Joseph Smith and The Church of Jesus Christ of Latter-day Saints.

Common Themes of the Twenty Visions

See key below	1	2	3	4	5	6	7
Joseph Smith Jr.	*	*	*	*	*	*	*
Benjamin Pomeroy	*	*		*			*
Isaiah Pratt	*	*					*
Daniel Rogers	*	*				*	
Joseph Bean	*	*	*				
Benjamin Abbott	*	*	*	*			*
Thomas Rankin	*	*	*				*
Lorenzo Dow	*	*				*	
Caleb Rich	*	*	*	*	*		
Elias Smith	*	*	*				
Nathan Culver	*	*	*				*
Sarah Alley	*	*					
Hannah Coy	*	*		*		*	*
Nathan Barlow	*	*	*	*			*
Norris Stearns	*	*	*	*	*		
Charles G. Finney	*	*	*				
Asa Wild	*	*		*	*		
Francis G. Bishop	*	*	*				
Billy Hibbard	*	*	*	*			
John Murdock	*	*	*	*			

Key

1. Saw God and/or Jesus Christ
2. Saw God & Christ as men
3. Vision came due to prayer or trial
4. Specific instruction related
5. Told no true church existed
6. Under 15 years of age
7. Evil influence present prior to the vision

Chapter Two

An Apostasy and Restoration Culture

Jesus Christ told Joseph Smith Jr. in the spring of 1820 that he must not join any church because they were all wrong: "all their creeds are an abomination in my sight. . . . Their hearts are far from me [and] they teach for doctrines the commandments of men, having a form of Godliness but they deny the power thereof."[46] This commandment prohibiting Joseph from joining a church due to corruption will be discussed at length in this chapter.

The previous statement that Latter-day Saints attribute to Christ offends Christians, especially Protestants. Note, however, that the Prophet Joseph did not preach animosity toward fellow Christians throughout his ministry. He taught that Christians of other faiths are good people who teach truth but have allowed error and falsehoods to creep into their doctrines. "Have the Presbyterians any truth?" he asked. "Yes. Have the Baptists, Methodists, etc., any truth? Yes. They all have a little truth mixed with error. We should gather all the good and true principles in the world and treasure them up, or we shall not come out true 'Mormons.' "[47] The Prophet also taught, "Rail not against the sects, neither talk against their tenets. But preach Christ and him crucified, love to God, and love to man."[48] Consider also his teaching on another occasion: "We ought always to be aware of those prejudices which sometimes so strangely present themselves, and are so congenial to human nature, against our friends, neighbors, and brethren of the world, who choose to differ from us in opinion and in matters of faith. Our religion is between us and our God. Their religion is between them and their God."[49]

That the Prophet Joseph did not believe all Christian sects were evil but that they lacked the necessary ordinances, authority, and apostolic succession is clear. Latter-day Saint doctrine affirms that an apostasy from Christ's original Church followed the death of Jesus and his Apostles. Latter-day Saint doctrine also affirms that Christ's Church was restored in the nineteenth century. Most people, both inside and outside the Church of Jesus Christ of Latter-day Saints, assume that Latter-day Saints are alone in teaching of an apostasy and restoration. This is not the case! Many Christians at different stages throughout history, but especially in Joseph Smith's generation, believed in an apostasy and the need for a restoration of Christ's original Church.

Apostasy and Christians

Regarding the belief in an apostasy among Protestant Christians, biblical and early Christian scholar Stephen Robinson, a Latter-day Saint, explained,

> It is surprising that Protestants would criticize the Latter-day Saints for believing in an apostasy and rejecting subsequent developments, since Protestants have essentially done the same thing—only instead of rejecting the authority of the traditional church after the first century, they reject it after the fifteenth. Protestant Reformers used many of the same Bible passages . . . to prove that the Roman church was corrupt and to justify their own attempts at reform. . . . If some Protestants argue that Mormons aren't Christians because they reject the Council of Nicaea (A.D. 325), couldn't Catholics argue that Protestants aren't Christians because they reject the Council of Trent (A.D. 1545–47)? . . . Thus, in terms of the doctrine of an apostasy—that is, that at some point in time the historical church was no longer the true

> Church—most Protestants agree with the Latter-day Saints in principle; they just differ on the dates.[50]

Robinson articulated that both Latter-day Saints and Protestants believe that during a certain point in history, Christ's Church was no longer on the earth. One of these Protestant Christians was Martin Luther (1483–1546). Luther began his study of theology in his early twenties and later became an Augustinian monk. In 1510, Luther traveled to Rome. He became critical of the Catholic Church and was especially disgusted with some of its teachings and practices. Indulgences and their corruption, according to Luther, of sacramental ordinances disturbed him the most. In an attempt to combat these heresies, Luther nailed his now famous Ninety-Five Theses to the door of the Castle Church in Wittenberg, Germany, in October 1517. The Catholic Church excommunicated Luther and labeled him a heretic. Many followers of Luther began calling themselves Lutherans. In response, Luther stated, "I pray you leave my name alone and call yourselves not 'Lutherans' but 'Christians.' Who is Luther? My teaching is not mine. I have not been crucified for anyone. . . . How then does it befit me, a miserable bag of dust and ashes, to give my name to the children of Christ? Cease, my dear friends, to cling to these party names and distinctions; away with them all; let us call ourselves only 'Christians' after Him from whom our teaching comes."[51] Luther recognized an important principle later taught in the Book of Mormon:

> Therefore, whatsoever ye shall do, ye shall do it in my name; therefore ye shall call the church in my name; and ye shall call upon the Father in my name that he will bless the church for my sake.
>
> And how be it my church save it be called in my name? For if a church be called in Moses' name then it be Moses' church; or if it be called in the name of a man then it be the church of a man; but if it be called in my name then it is my church, if it so be that they are built upon my gospel. (3 Nephi 27:7–8)

Throughout his ministry, Luther diverted attention away

from himself and placed it on Jesus Christ. One of Luther's main objectives during his life was to *restore* true Christianity.[52]

William Tyndale (1494–1536), another well known religious reformer and scholar, sacrificed much of his life studying the doctrines of the scriptures and translating the Bible into English. Referring to a falling away from Christ's Church, Tyndale wrote, "they that had the plough by the tail looked back, the plough went awry; faith waxed feeble and fainty; love waxed cold; the scriptures waxed dark; Christ was no more seen."[53] John Wesley (1703–1791), founder of Methodism, also referred to a falling away from Christ's Church, as well as a loss of spiritual gifts among Christians, "It does not appear that these extraordinary gifts of the Holy Ghost were common in the Church for more than two or three centuries. We seldom hear of them after that fatal period when the Emperor Constantine called himself a Christian. . . . From this time they almost totally ceased. . . . The extraordinary gifts of the Holy Ghost were no longer to be found in the Christian Church; because the Christians were turned Heathens again, and had only a dead form left."[54] Speaking of the latter days Wesley stated, "The times which we have reason to believe are at hand, (if they are not already begun) are what pious men have termed '*the latter day glory*'; meaning the time wherein God would gloriously display his power and love in the fulfillment of his gracious promise that 'the knowledge of the Lord shall cover the earth, as the waters cover the sea.' "[55] Wesley preached this sermon in the late eighteenth century, a short time

John Wesley

preceding the birth of Joseph Smith and the establishment of God's latter-day kingdom.

Concerning an apostasy of the first-century Church, Roger Williams (1603–1684), a Baptist theologian, concluded that there occurred "a total routing of the Church and Ministry of Christ Jesus, put to flight, and retired into the Wilderness of Desolation," and that it would not return until God once again commissioned apostles and prophets like the days of old.[56] On another occasion Williams opined that "There is no regularly constituted church on earth, nor any person authorized to administer any church ordinance; nor can there be *until new apostles are sent by the Great Head of the Church* for whose coming I am seeking."[57] United Minister Pierre Van Paassen (1895–1968) similarly recognized a need for apostles and prophets in the last days: "A world without prophets is a world that knows not its signs. It is like a ship without rudder or compass floundering about helplessly, aimlessly drifting toward perdition."[58]

Harry Emerson Fosdick (1878–1969) a Baptist minister from Buffalo, New York, was concerned that Christianity had become largely an organization of mythologies and creeds that Christ already rejected.

> A religious reformation is afoot, and at heart it is the endeavor to recover for our modern life the religion of Jesus as against the vast, intricate, largely inadequate and often positively false religion about Jesus. Christianity today has largely left the religion which he preached, taught and lived, and has substituted another kind of religion altogether. If Jesus should come back to earth now, hear the mythologies built up around him, see the creedalism, denominationalism, sacramentalism, carried on in his name, he would certainly say, "If this is Christianity, I am not a Christian."[59]

Philosopher and author Ralph Waldo Emerson (1803–1882) was born into the Unitarian faith of which his father was a minister. He soon became disaffected with their doctrines. While speaking to students at Harvard Divinity School Emerson said, "It is my duty to say to you that the need was never greater [for] new revelation than now. The doctrine of inspiration is lost. . . . Men have come to speak of . . . revelation as somewhat long ago given and done, as if God were dead. . . . It is the office of a true teacher to show us that God is, not was; that He speaketh, not spake."[60]

In the late eighteenth century, Elias Smith (mentioned in the previous chapter) saw a vision of the Savior standing atop mount Zion. During this vision, he learned that all denominations of Christianity were in error. Smith struggled in knowing exactly what God wanted him to do. "My mind was ensnared," he recalled, "and I felt myself in a situation from which it was not in my power to extricate myself. I found that my mind was still entangled with the old *Calvinistic doctrine*, and that about all the difference between *Calvinism* and *Universalism* was in the number." He subsequently prayed for guidance and described hearing a "gentile [*sic*] whisper" commanding him to "drop them both and search the scriptures." In 1805, Smith left the ministry as a Baptist minister and established a movement called the Church of Christ. Smith believed that his church was the only one that possessed the truth of Christ.[61]

Alexander Campbell

In 1820, shortly following the organization and subsequent collapse of Elias Smith's restoration movement, a Presbyterian minister named Barton W. Stone left his ministry and founded his own *Springfield Presbytery* movement. Stone's primary objective was to "*restore apostolic Christianity*." He later merged with a similar movement led by Thomas and Alexander Campbell.[62] This movement, of which Sidney Rigdon was a key figure before joining with Joseph Smith, also sought to restore primitive Christianity. "Some new revelation," stated Alexander Campbell, "or some new development of the revelation of God must be made. . . . *We want the old gospel back* that is sustained by the *ancient order of things*."[63] Speaking of the corruption in Christianity, Campbell wrote, "We argue that all Christian sects are more or less apostatized from the institutions of the Savior: that by all the obligations of the Christian religion, they that fear and love the Lord are bound to [see] . . . a *restoration of the ancient order of things*."[64]

The difference between Joseph Smith and Alexander Campbell regarding a restoration was their view on authority. As one non-LDS historian observed, Joseph Smith viewed himself as called of God to usher in the restoration of that "golden age of direct revelation." Alexander Campbell, on the other hand, claimed that one received authority through the Bible and that restoring the primitive gospel would be rational to anyone who understood the Bible.[65] Note that Campbell preached heavily concerning a restoration of the ancient gospel while Joseph Smith was in the process of restoring the ancient gospel.

John H. Noyes

In 1831, John H. Noyes of Vermont attended Yale Theological Seminary to become a minister. He preached that the Second Coming of Christ had already passed. He taught that Christ returned in AD 70, the year of the destruction of the Jerusalem temple. He also taught that the re-establishment of God's kingdom was imminent. Shortly after Joseph Smith organized the Church of Jesus Christ in 1830, Noyes prophetically stated that a church on earth "*is now rising to meet the approaching kingdom in the heavens, and to become its duplicate and representative on earth . . . and the men who usher in the kingdom of God, will be guided, not merely by theoretical truth, but by the Spirit of God.*" Noyes most likely had not encountered the Mormons up to this point, which makes his prophecy much more intriguing for Latter-day Saints. In 1848, Noyes established the Oneida Community in Oneida, New York. His movement sought to restore the church that Christ had established during his earthly ministry. Noyes died in 1886 and the Oneida Community dwindled shortly thereafter.[66]

A few Catholic popes and theologians have also recognized a problem with corruption in Christianity and the succession of apostles. "We know well," stated Pope Adrian VI (1459–1523), "that for many years things deserving of abhorrence have gathered round. . . . Sacred things have been misused, ordinances transgressed, so that in everything there has been a change for the worse. Thus, it is not surprising that the malady has crept down from the head to the members, from the popes to the hierarchy. We all, prelates and clergy, have gone astray from the right way."[67] Consider also the following statement of a Catholic theologian who, after careful study of the apostolic succession of Christ's apostles, said, "One conclusion seems obvious: Neither the New Testament nor early Christian history offers support for a notion of apostolic succession as an *unbroken line of episcopal ordination from Christ through the apostles down through the centuries to the bishops of today.*"[68]

Orson F. Whitney recounted a discussion that he had with a Catholic theologian regarding apostolic succession.

> I bear in mind another noted visitor, a great scholar, who came here many years after the advent of the railroad. I became well acquainted with him, and we had more than one conversation together. I admired his vast erudition. He seemed to know all about law, literature, science, philosophy, and had a dozen languages at his tongue's end. He said to me one day: "You Mormons are all ignoramuses. You don't even know the strength of

> your own position. It is so strong that there is only one other tenable in the whole Christian world, and that is the position of the Roman Catholic Church. *The issue is between Mormonism and Catholicism. If you are right, we are wrong. If we are right, you are wrong. And that's all there is to it.* These Protestant sects haven't a leg to stand on; for if we are right, we cut them off long ago as apostates; and if we are wrong, they are wrong with us, for they were part of us and came out of us. *If we have the apostolic succession from St. Peter as we claim, there was no need for Joseph Smith and Mormonism; but if we have not that succession, such a man as Joseph Smith was necessary and Mormonism's position is the only consistent one. It is either the perpetuation of the gospel from ancient times, or the restoration of the gospel in latter days.*"[69]

Thomas Jefferson (1743–1826) recognized the need for a restoration of the ancient gospel. "The religion builders," wrote Jefferson, "have so distorted and deformed the doctrines of Jesus, so muffled them in mysticisms, fancies and falsehoods, have caricatured them into forms so inconceivable—as to shock reasonable thinkers."[70] Jefferson also stated that he was "Happy in the prospect of a *restoration of primitive Christianity*," and that he felt he "must leave to younger persons to encounter and lop off the false branches which have been engrafted into it by the mythologists of the middle and modern ages."[71] Six years before his death, Jefferson opined that "If the freedom of religion . . . can ever rise in practice under the overbearing inquisition of public opinion, *truth will prevail over fanaticism, and the genuine doctrines of Jesus. . . will again be restored to their original purity.*" This restoration, he stated, "will advance with the other improvements of the human mind, but too late for me to witness it."[72]

Perhaps the most striking statement of Jefferson regarding a restoration was also written six years before his death: "The genuine and simple religion of Jesus *will one day be restored*: such as it was preached and practiced by himself. Very soon after his death it became muffled up in mysteries, and has been ever since kept in concealment from the vulgar eye."[73] Jefferson offered these two statements in 1820, the same year in which Joseph Smith saw the

First Vision. Jefferson stated that when the doctrines of Jesus were "restored," it would be too late for him "to witness it." He died in 1826, just four years prior to the organization of the Church of Jesus Christ. Note that Jefferson's idea of a restoration was different than what Latter-day Saints today define as *restoration* that involves the spirit of prophecy and the spirit of revelation.

America was divinely guided in its establishment and founded upon religious principles that were taught and practiced by primitive Christians and Jews. The Constitution of the United States was essentially proof that America had entered a covenant with God. Several figures that help found the United States of America believed that the establishment of America was the beginning of the restored *order of the ages*. Consequently, they associated themselves with many of the customs and practices of the ancient Israelites. For instance, certain groups attempted to make Hebrew the official language of the newly founded nation[74] and many towns were named after those found in the Bible (for example, *Salem*, New Hampshire, Massachusetts, and Virginia; *Jericho*, Vermont; *Hebron*, Connecticut; *Goshen*, New Hampshire; *Bethlehem*, New York and Pennsylvania; *Damascus*, Virginia; *Bethel*, Connecticut; *Old Canaan*, Connecticut).

One non-LDS scholar who specializes in eighteenth- and nineteenth-century restoration movements has highlighted the "popularity of the restoration vision in early nineteenth-century America" and said that the idea of restoring primitive Christianity was "an important theme built into the heart and soul of American culture in the early nineteenth century."[75] He also explained that the seal of the United States carries the message of a restoration as follows:

> The great seal of the United States makes precisely the same point. There, an unfinished pyramid grows from arid desert sands. Inscribed on the pyramid's base is that notable date, 1776. Clearly, the pyramid represents a new nation. The barren desert terrain, above which the pyramid towers and from which it seems to grow, signifies all human history prior to 1776. For all their

> glories and achievements, past civilizations were essentially barren compared to the glories that would mark the new American state. The pyramid is unfinished since other nations have not yet emulated the American example and thrown off the yoke of tyranny. But as the American example penetrates the dark places of the world and as nation after nation and tribe after tribe rise up and reject the rule of tyrants, the world will become increasingly free, and when the world is free, the Millennium will have dawned. God clearly approves of this vision since above the pyramid we find his eye and, above that eye, the Latin phrase *annuit coeptis*, "He has smiled on our beginnings." And beneath the pyramid stands the most critical phrase of all, *novus ordo seclorum*, "a new order of the ages."[76]

Christians throughout the world since the passing of the New Testament Apostles believed that the Church established by Jesus was no longer on the earth and that a restoration was necessary. Restorationism was not prevalent among just a few religious groups or social classes but among everyone. One restorationist stated in 1830 that discussions and sermons regarding restorationism, millennialism, and the latter-day glory was "heard all over the land, and men [were] required to use all their exertions to usher in the glory of the last days, by converting the world."[77] Another scholar, in commenting on the culture of antebellum America, wrote that restorationism, millennialism, and biblicism was "truly so omnipresent in the American culture of 1800 or 1820 that historians have as much difficulty taking cognizance of it as of the air people breathed."[78] In 1848, after reading articles and statements of faith of fifty-three American religions, John W. Nevin concluded that discussions of restoring primitive Christianity was the major feature of American religion before the Civil War.[79]

Woman seen by John the Revelator in vision

Apostasy and Nineteenth-Century Restoration Culture

The interpretation of biblical prophecies was a major component of restorationism that seemed to peak during the Second Great Awakening. People of every religious demographic, especially theologians and preachers, justified a restoration using certain biblical prophecies, usually from the books of Daniel and Revelation. It was common to find interpretations of these prophecies in books, pamphlets, sermons, magazines, and newspapers.[80] A process referred to as *prophetic numerology* helped interpret the prophecies. The following explanation may be helpful.

In Revelation 12:1–14, John the Revelator recorded a vision he saw of a woman wearing a crown containing twelve stars. The woman was pregnant with a "man child" who would eventually rule "all nations with a rod of iron" (vv. 2–5). John saw that the woman would flee into the "wilderness" and return after "twelve-hundred and sixty days" (vv. 6, 14). Joseph Smith, as well as many other biblical commentators in the eighteenth and nineteenth centuries, interpreted John's vision to mean that the "woman," who represents "Christ's Church," would flee into the "wilderness," which represents apostasy. The Prophet Joseph explained that the Church would not return until the passing of a 1,260-day apostasy. In Joseph Smith's Translation of the Bible, "days" was changed to "years" (see JST Revelation 12:6).[81] Daniel 7:18–25 contains a similar prophecy explaining that in the last days the "saints of the most High" and the "kingdom" of God would be restored after 1,260 days. While Revelation 12:6 states, "twelve-hundred and sixty days" (NRSV), Revelation 12:14 states, "a time, and times, and a half a time." Daniel 7:25 similarly designated the length of the apostasy as, "a time and times and the dividing of time." What does this mean? "Time" refers to one year, "times" refers to two years, and "a dividing of time" or "a half a time" refers to one-half of a year, totaling three and one-half years. Notice that three and one-half years equals 1,260 days. In scripture, "twelve hundred and sixty days" or three and one-half years, symbolized a period of time that was limited. Three and one-half is half of seven. Note that the number seven symbolizes completeness, wholeness, and perfection. Thus, three and one-half is not complete but "arrested midway in its normal course." Therefore, when John the Revelator saw that the Church would flee into wilderness and return after "twelve hundred and sixty days," he understood that to mean the Church would flee into apostasy for a limited time, and Satan, in his attempts to destroy the Church, would be "arrested midway in its normal course."[82]

Many biblical scholars understood *days* or *times* to mean "years," based on at least two passages in the Bible:

> I have laid upon thee *the years of their iniquity, according to the number of the days,* three hundred and ninety days: so shalt thou bear the iniquity of the house of Israel.
>
> And when thou hast accomplished them . . . thou shalt bear the iniquity of the house of Judah forty days: *I have appointed thee each day for a year.*" (Ezekiel 4:5–6; emphasis added)

> And your children shall wander in the wilderness forty years, and bear your whoredoms, until your carcases be wasted in the wilderness.
>
> After the number of the days in which ye searched the land, *even forty days, each day for a year,* shall ye bear your iniquities, even forty years, and ye shall know my breach of promise." (Numbers 14:34; emphasis added)

Although some understood "twelve hundred and sixty years" to be figurative, many Christians throughout the centuries interpreted it literally. It seemed clear that these prophecies state that Christ's Church would enter into apostasy and then be restored after 1,260 years. So, according to these Christians, when did the 1,260-year apostasy begin? They understood that the apostasy began with the arrival of the "antichrist," the "dragon" in Revelation 12 and the "beasts" and "kings" in Daniel 7. Fascinating, at least for Latter-day Saints, is that many Christians believed that the "antichrist" appeared when the Lombards, a Germanic people from Northern Europe, invaded Rome in AD 570,[83] thus causing the Church to flee into the wilderness for 1260 years until 1830! Other Christians believed that the birth of the prophet Muhammad and the rise of Islam, or the rise of medieval papacy (office of pope) beginning with the career of Gregory the Great, signified the arrival of the "antichrist."[84] Note that the birth of Muhammed and the rise of papacy in the Catholic Church also occurred in AD 570, placing the return of the Church, or Restoration in 1830. The end of the sixth century AD is significant in the history of Christianity because it marks the beginning of the appropriately titled "Dark Ages."

Keep in mind that neither the Catholic Church nor Islam is the "antichrist." A large majority of Muslims are good people. They try to live by the teachings of the Prophet Muhammed, who taught his followers to display charity and peace. It is uncertain as to who exactly is the "antichrist." The Apostle John explained that the "antichrist" is anyone, or any organization who denies Jesus Christ (see 1 John 2:22; 1 John 4:3; 2 John 1:7). Clearly, Catholics do not reject Christ, and neither do Muslims. Islam venerates Jesus and views him as a great prophet but not an Atoner and Savior.

John Calvin

Virtually every eighteenth- and nineteenth-century theologian who published an interpretation of the relevant biblical prophecies placed the Apostasy sometime between 533 CE and 606 CE, which means they believed that the 1,260-year apostasy would end, depending on their interpretation, sometime in the first half of the nineteenth century. One Christian who believed that the Church fell into apostasy in AD 570 was the well-known reformer, John Calvin (1509–1564). Commenting on these events, as well as on Paul's prophecy of a "falling away" (2 Thessalonians 2:1–8), Calvin wrote,

> We may at once conclude how useful this prediction of Paul's is. For it might have seemed that a building [the Christian Church] which . . . lay for so long in ruins, could not have been the work of God had Paul not warned them long before, that this would take place. . . . Paul, however, is not speaking of one individual but of a kingdom that was to be seized by Satan for the purpose of setting up a seat of abomination in the midst of God's temple. *This we see accomplished in Popery. . . . The sect of Mohammed [570f A.D.]* was like a raging overflow which in its violence *tore away about half of the Church.* It remained for Antichrist to infect the part which was left.[85]

Notice that Calvin believed that the Catholic popes and the "sect of Mohammed" were not the antichrist, but that the antichrist would "infect" the portion of the Church that had not already been torn away by the popes and the "sect of Mohammed."

Biblical scholar and Methodist theologian Adam Clarke (1762–1832), speaking of the decline of Rome and the Church falling into apostasy, stated, "The establishment of the Lombards in Italy [AD 570] was more likely to produce the utter subversion of the Christian Church than the irruptions of so many barbarous nations into the Roman empire."[86] In 1847, Edward Elliot explained why the fall of the Roman Empire caused the Great Apostasy. A few years after the Lombard conquest in AD 570, concluded Elliott, "The Emperor Phocas confirmed the right of the Roman . . . Bishop to the Headship of all churches," which only invited corruption. This, he concluded, was just another sign "*of commencement to the 1260 years.*"[87] Reverend John Dowling further explained that before Emperor Phocas, "the bishop of Rome had no power to enforce his decisions upon other churches and bishops. Now by the sovereign decrees of his holiness, the Pope, all must be conformed to the [new] standard or be branded with the name of heretics."[88]

In 1809, a magazine published by the Friends of Evangelical Truth printed the following interpretation of the 1,260-year apostasy: "*This period of twelve hundred and sixty years is the duration of the great apostasy* in its dominant state, or the reign of the two little horns of the beast, one in the East, and the other in the West, or Mohammedism and Popery. *These two apostate horns arose together in the same year [A.D. 570]*, and will continue to depress the church to the time of the end."[89] In his 1829 biblical commentary, Philip Allwood explained that the "North of Italy falling under the dominion of the Lombards [AD 570] *commenced the period of the one thousand two hundred and sixty years*; and the first decisive overt-acts of the two great Systems of the *Apostasy*."[90] Thus we see, according to the aforementioned Christian accounts, how the Church was corrupted.

Like many other theologians, Martin Luther believed in the necessity of a restoration of primitive Christianity. He said, "I persuade myself verily, that the [Church] *will not be absent full three hundred years*. God will not, can not, suffer this wicked world much longer. The great day is drawing near in which the kingdom of abominations shall be overthrown."[91] Note that Luther wrote this statement during his ministry, sometime between 1510 and 1546, which would place the return of the Church, according to Luther, sometime between 1810 and 1846.

Although John Calvin, Adam Clarke, Edward Elliot, Philip Allwood, and the Friends of Evangelical Truth did not specifically state that the Church would return in 1830, it is clear that they believed that the 1,260-year apostasy began in AD 570. One scholar who did specifically state that the Restoration of the Church would occur in 1830 was Reverend William Ward of the Church of England. Sometime between 1810 and 1820, Ward wrote,

> In 568 the Lombard invasion began, and in three years intercepted all communication between Rome and the Exarchate, by which the popes became sole masters of Rome and acquired all the civil and military power, as well as spiritual authority in the city, A.D. 570. . . . But having traced the first exercise of independent temporal sovereignty by the pope from A.D. 570, I propose the following test of my opinion. . . . The 1260 years will also coincide with this conclusion . . . by reckoning from the pope's temporal dominion in Rome, in consequence of the Lombard invasion, 570 to 1830.[92]

Ward also concluded that the year of 1830 would be "a year of spiritual revival and triumph, the greatest year in the calendar of the world."[93] Another scholar who recognized 1830 as a monumental year in history of Christianity was Errett Gates, who wrote in 1905, "It is apparent by the year 1830 that a new period has dawned in the movement for the union of all Christians by the restoration of primitive Christianity."[94] Although Gates was referring to the work of Alexander Campbell and the Disciples of Christ in restoring primitive Christianity, it is significant that he recognized 1830 as the year of the fulfillment of the prophecies and a turning point for Christ's Church. In 1830, Adam Clarke reported that people were beginning to experience an increase of the Holy Ghost and that "never were there times more favorable; never were spiritual advantages more numerous; never was light more abundant" than during this generation.[95]

Latter-day Saint documents show that Joseph Smith and the Saints knew of these predictions by other Christians. The *Times and Seasons* reported, "We are informed by the renowned historian, Whelpley . . . that the church of Jesus Christ was overrun, and driven into the wilderness, A.D. 570, and John the Revelator informs us it must remain there 1260 years, which makes exactly the time, the year 1830, that the Church of Jesus Christ of Latter day Saints was organized, with the gifts and blessings."[96] In a later issue, the *Times and Seasons* offered the following commentary on Revelation 12:5 in a series of questions and answers: "What was the rod? A. It was the power and priesthood after the holy order of the son of God, which the church had; and was delivered of it, or rather, *it was taken from her in the year 570, and the church fell into the hands of the Pope of Rome*."[97]

Since the year 1830 is a theme of this chapter, the visionary account of Margaret Macdonald is worth mentioning here. *The Restoration of Apostles and Prophets in the Catholic Apostolic Church*, published in 1861, recounted a vision seen in early 1830 by fifteen-year-old Margaret Macdonald of Scotland. One afternoon while listening to a sermon on the last days, Margaret saw a vision that she later related to her minister. It was recorded that she saw a "people of God" who were now waiting for the "sign of the Son of Man" and that soon, a "glorious temple" was "about to be reared." Macdonald also saw that there would soon "be an outpouring of the Spirit on the body [of the Church], such as has not been [before]" and that God wished "all should be filled."[98]

Questions that must be explored regarding the *restoration culture* of the nineteenth century are: How widespread were discussions of restorationism and prophetic numerology? Were they discussed by only a select few? If so, who? Were these topics explored by people of every Christian denomination? In 1810, Reverend Samuel Davies answered these questions when he stated that not everyone agreed on the exact date when the Church would return but that "it is generally agreed, that we are not far from the end of it."[99] Another scholar of nineteenth-century restorationism stated that between the years of 1790 and 1840, discussions of biblical prophecy and a restoration were salient among all groups, not just ministers and theologians.[100] Biblical scholar William Cuninghame agreed when he wrote in 1843 that from 1828 to 1833, "a greater number of tracts and works on the subject of the advent and declaring its nearness went forth to the public and . . . in the leading religious journals of the day than had previously appeared in any whole century, in the whole period that had elapsed from the age of the apostles."[101] In 1828, minister and biblical scholar Robert Reid explained that virtually all of his fellow Protestant ministers and biblical commentators, as well as many Catholics, believed that the 1,260-year apostasy would end in their generation.[102]

The previous statements and accounts are quite fascinating. Many people do not realize that Latter-day Saints are not the only people who have taught, and continue to teach, the occurrence of an apostasy. Hundreds of biblical commentaries, books, and pamphlets published in the eighteenth and nineteenth centuries discussed *prophetic numerology* and claimed that Christ's Church fell into apostasy during the late sixth century and, therefore, was restored sometime during the early- to mid-nineteenth century.

Visions, Apostasy, and a Restoration

Information in the previous sections, when coupled with the accounts in this section, provides a clearer picture into the restoration culture in which the Lord chose to reestablish his Church. It seems that the idea of a restoration spread rapidly as the Lord began to enlighten the minds of people to prepare them for his latter-day work. This section contains nine accounts of individuals who were told in dreams or visions that all religious sects were in error, or that in a short time, God would restore his Church to the earth. All of the manifestations occurred during this restoration generation of the late eighteenth and early nineteenth centuries.

The first of these individuals is Caleb Rich of Warwick, Massachusetts, who was raised a Baptist but converted to Universalism after seeing a vision in 1772. One day, Rich heard "*a still small voice*" that said to him, "your motive is from selfish principles, for fear of future and endless misery; you always have been and now are excited to pray from the same false motives." At that moment, he saw a "celestial" being who told him he was a "stone" that was "placed by unerring wisdom into God's building *before the foundation of the world*." Rich followed this "celestial" being to "Mount Zion" where he was commanded to avoid the Baptists. When they reached the summit, Rich saw "the house of

God and the gate of heaven." Instantly, the vision closed. Rich never returned to the Baptist Church but joined the Universalists. He soon became influential in that church and was eventually ordained a New England Universalist leader. One evening in April 1778, Rich saw another vision just after retiring to bed. He saw "a person, or the likeness of one" enter his room carrying a bible. The personage quoted verses from the New Testament and then stated, "*There [is] not one formal church among them . . . that stood in the Apostolic rectitude or that contended for the Faith once delivered to the saints.*" He was instructed to "proclaim the same gospel" that Christ preached.[103]

Robert Mason, resident of Sainsbury, Connecticut, and family friend of the Woodruffs, was considered by many to be a prophet. In 1800, Mason saw the Restoration of the gospel in vision and later related it to Wilford Woodruff, who learned of the vision in 1830. Woodruff described Mason's experience in his journal.

> The last time I ever saw him he related to me the following vision, which he had in his field in open day: "I was carried away in a vision and found myself in the midst of a vast orchard of fruit trees. I became hungry and wandered through this vast orchard searching for fruit to eat, but I found none. While I stood in amazement finding no fruit in the midst of so many trees, they began to fall to the ground as if torn up by a whirlwind. They continued to fall until there was not a tree standing in the whole orchard. I immediately saw thereafter shoots springing up from the roots and forming themselves into young and beautiful trees. These budded, blossomed, and brought forth fruit, which ripened and was the most beautiful to look upon of anything my eyes had ever beheld. I stretched forth my hand and plucked some of the fruit. I gazed upon it with delight; but when I was about to eat of it, the vision closed and I did not taste the fruit. At the close of the vision I bowed down in humble prayer and asked the Lord to show me the meaning of the vision. Then the voice of the Lord came to me saying: 'Son of man, thou hast sought me diligently to know the truth concerning my Church and Kingdom among men. This is to show you that *my Church is not organized among men in the generation to which you belong; but in the days of your children the Church and Kingdom of God shall be made manifest*

> *with all the gifts and the blessings enjoyed by the Saints in past ages.* You shall live to be made acquainted with it, but shall not partake of its blessings before you depart this life. You will be blest of the Lord after death because you have followed the dictation of my Spirit in this life.'"
>
> When Father Mason had finished relating the vision and its interpretation, he said, calling me by my name: "Wilford, I shall never partake of this fruit in the flesh, but you will and you will become a conspicuous actor in the new kingdom." He then turned and left me. These were the last words he ever spoke to me upon the earth. To me this was a very striking circumstance. I had passed many days during a period of twenty years with this old Father Mason. He had never mentioned this vision to me before. On this occasion he said he felt impelled by the Spirit of the Lord to relate it to me.[104]

This vision caused Woodruff to search for the same organization that governed Christ's New Testament Church. He also searched for a church who manifested "all the gifts and the blessings enjoyed by the Saints in past ages." When Woodruff first encountered Mormon missionaries in 1833, he did not hesitate to join the Church.

In 1810, Chloe Willey of Goshen, New Hampshire, published visions she saw of the last days in which an angelic personage explained the Restoration to her as follows:

> In the glorious day, which was shortly to take place, *the purity of Christ's church should be established*; that miracles should be wrought by his faithful servants; that cripples, with those possessed with diseases, might be restored, which this angel told me, must be done by anointing them with oil in the name of the Lord, and the prayers of two godly persons, or ministers; and that they must have faith, and in that day the Lord would do great things for Zion, and her watchmen should be of one mind. . . . He said, *the time shall shortly come, when the stone, cut out of the mountain, without hands, which we read of in Daniel II. 34 and 35, should become great, and fill the whole earth*; that there would be glorious days in America; and that Christ should be their king, and reign from the rising sun to the setting sun.[105]

Willey recorded that the restoration of miracles and healing would soon occur. In addition, these miracles and healings would be performed by at least "two godly persons" who would "anoint" the sick with "oil" in the "name of the Lord." On February 9, 1831, just twenty-one years after Willey's vision, the Lord told Joseph Smith in a revelation: "And the elders of the church, two or more, shall be called, and shall pray for and lay their hands upon them in my name" (D&C 42:44). Since that revelation, thousands of accounts of miraculous healings and even raisings of the dead have been recorded by Latter-day Saints.[106] The angel also told Willey that the prophecy in Daniel 2 that speaks of God's Church (the stone cut out of the mountains without hands) filling the "whole earth," would soon be fulfilled. Regarding this prophecy Joseph Smith taught,

> I will correct the idea in regard to the little stone rolling forth, as foretold in Daniel, chapter 2. This is not so. It is stationary, like a grind stone, and revolves. (He made a motion with his hands showing how it turned.) When the Elders go abroad to preach the gospel, and the people become believers in the Book of Mormon and are baptized, they are added to the little stone. Thus, they are gathered around it so that it grows larger and larger until it begins to pinch the toes of the image, and finally breaks it into pieces to be carried away like the chaff of a summer's threshing, while the stone will keep growing until it fills the whole earth.[107]

Joseph Smith Sr., as mentioned previously, also had significant dreams and visions. Specifically, his wife Lucy recorded seven manifestations from 1811 to 1819.[108] The two most significant manifestations were his visions of the Restoration and the tree of life similar to Lehi's account in the Book of Mormon. At the time, Joseph Smith Sr. had not joined a church, as he felt that none of them fit the organization that Christ established during his ministry. He sought for a church that was patterned after "*the ancient order*, as established by our Lord and Savior, Jesus Christ, and his apostles." His first manifestation took place in Tunbridge, Vermont, in April 1811.

> I seemed to be traveling in an open, barren field, and as I was traveling, I turned my eyes towards the east, the west, the north and the south, but could see nothing save dead, fallen timber. Not a vestige of life, either animal or vegetable, could be seen; besides, to render the scene still more dreary, the most death-like silence prevailed, no sound of anything animate could be heard in all the field. I was alone in this gloomy desert, with the exception of an attendant spirit, who kept constantly by my side. Of him I inquired the meaning of what I saw, and why I was thus traveling in such a dismal place. He answered thus: "T*his field is the world, which now lieth inanimate and dumb, in regard to the true religion, or plan of salvation*; but travel on, and by the wayside you will find on a certain log a box, the contents of which, if you eat thereof, will make you wise, and give unto you wisdom and understanding." I carefully observed what was told me by my guide, and proceeding a short distance, I came to the box. I immediately took it up, and placed it under my left arm; then with eagerness I raised the lid, and began to taste of its contents; upon which all manner of beasts, horned cattle, and roaring animals, rose up on every side in the most threatening manner possible, tearing the earth, tossing their horns, and bellowing most terrifically all around me, and they finally came so close upon me, that I was compelled to drop the box and fly for my life. Yet, in the midst of all this I was perfectly happy, though I awoke trembling.[109]

Regarding her husband's vision, Lucy Mack Smith recorded, "From this forward my husband seemed more confirmed than ever in the opinion that there was no order or class of religionists that knew any more concerning the Kingdom of God than those of the world, or such as made no profession of religion whatever."[110]

In 1815, just five years before Joseph's First Vision, Norris Stearns of Greenfield, Massachusetts, published a vision that he saw, as cited in the previous chapter. The latter portion of Stearns' account was reserved for this chapter because of the nature of the message. Following his description of what he saw and felt while experiencing a manifestation of God the Father and Jesus Christ, Stearns recorded that they gave him "*an introduction to a greater work that will soon be manifest; for the Angel that has the Everlasting Gospel to preach is coming . . . to do his work.*" Stearns claimed authority to deliver this message and considered himself a "prophet." He wrote, "By permission of the Lord God, whose servant and Prophet I am, I inform the people that *part of the 14th Chapter of Revelation is now fulfilling*: and that the Lord has already begun to deliver His People."[111] Notice, as stated in the conclusion to chapter 1, that even though Stearns claimed to be a prophet, he did not claim authority to restore the "Everlasting Gospel." He simply claimed authority to spread the word concerning a "greater work that will soon be manifest."

One year after Norris Stearns published his vision, Solomon Chamberlain, a Reformed Methodist from Old Canaan, Connecticut, recorded a remarkable vision. An angel told Chamberlain that no true church presently existed on earth and that the Lord would soon "raise up a church" with the "apostolic order." In 1830, fourteen years following his vision, Chamberlain met the Smith family and subsequently recorded his interaction with them. As Chamberlain related his vision to the Smith family, those present, including Hyrum, were overcome with emotion.

> The Lord showed me in a vision that there were *no people on the earth that were right, and that faith was gone from the earth, excepting a few, and that all churches were corrupt*. I further saw in the vision that *he would soon raise up a church that would be after the apostolic order*, that there would be in it the same powers and gifts that were in the days of Christ, and that I should live to see the day, and that there would [be] a book come forth, like unto the Bible, and the people would be guided by it, as well as the Bible. . . .
>
> [About 1830] I had occasion to go on a visit into Upper Canada . . . When the boat came to Palmyra, I felt as if some Genii or good spirit told me to leave the boat. This was a few miles from where the record [Book of Mormon] was found. After leaving the boat, the Spirit manifested to me to travel a south course. I did so for about 3 miles. . . . From the time I left the boat until now, I was wholly led by the Spirit or my Genii. I soon made my way across lots to Father Smith's and found Hyrum walking the floor as I entered the door. I said, "Peace be to this house."

> He [Hyrum Smith] looked at me as one astonished and said, "I hope it will be peace." I then said, "Is there anyone here that believes in visions and revelations?" He said, "Yes, we are a visionary house." I said, "Then I will give you one of my pamphlets, which was visionary and of my own experience." They then called the people together which consisted of 5 or 6 men who were out at the door. Father Smith was one and some of the Whitmer's. They then sat down and read my pamphlet. Hyrum read first, but was so affected, he could not read it. He then gave it to a man, which I learned was Christian Whitmer. He finished reading it. I then opened my mouth and began to preach to them in the words that the angel had made known to me in the vision, *that all churches and denominations on the earth had become corrupt and [that] no church of God [was] on the earth* but that he would shortly *raise up a church that would never be confounded or brought down, and be like unto the apostolic church.* They wondered greatly who had been telling me these things, for said they, we have the same things written down in our house, taken from the Gold record that you are preaching to us . . . I then said, "If you are a visionary house, I wish you would make known some of your discoveries, for I think I can bear them." They then made known to me that they had obtained a gold record and [had] just finished translating it. Now the Lord revealed to me by the gift and power of the Holy Ghost that this was the work I had been looking for. I stayed 2 days and they instructed me in the manuscripts of the Book of Mormon.[112]

Daniel Tyler, a Methodist from Springfield, Pennsylvania, related his grandfather's prophecy and visionary experience in 1823. At the time, Tyler's grandfather was not affiliated with a church. Tyler also related the event of his grandfather—following his death—appearing to his father.

> One day my father happened to open to Mark, 16th chapter, 16th and 17th verses. After reading them several times carefully he said, "There is not a true believer in the world," as the promise was that the signs spoken of should follow those who believed. He showed the passage to several ministers, mostly Methodists, and argued with them. The more he argued the more convinced he was that *the gospel was not on the earth*, and he was able to confound the most learned divines, although he was quite illiterate.

> My grandfather also had the same views and he *prophesied that he would die, but my father would live to see the true church organized with all the apostolic gifts and blessings*. . . .
>
> After my grandfather [became sick] with his last illness, he told my parents that an angel appeared to him clothed in white, and told him he would not recover, for his sickness was unto death. Ten days later he died. To save ridicule, however, this vision was kept secret and only told me afterwards by my mother.[113]

Several years later in 1832, Samuel Smith and Orson Hyde were preaching in the community. After hearing their message and reading the Book of Mormon, all but Tyler's parents requested baptism; his father seemed to be the most skeptical. Tyler recorded, "Soon after [my baptism], my grandfather appeared to my father in a dream, and told him *that this was the people he prophesied of while living*, and my parents were baptized."[114]

In 1830, Newel and Elizabeth Whitney, Campbellites from Kirtland, Ohio, searched desperately for a church that taught the doctrines of the Bible. They prayed that God would guide them to a church that manifested spiritual gifts and claimed authority to bestow the gift of the Holy Ghost. The Campbellites baptized for the remission of sins and taught that spiritual gifts were for the blessing of all people, but they did not claim authority to confer the gift of the Holy Ghost. One night while Newel and Elizabeth Whitney prayed, they saw a vision. Elizabeth recorded the event as follows:

> My husband and I were in our house at Kirtland, praying to the Father to be shown the way when the Spirit rested upon us and a cloud overshadowed the house. It was as though we were out of doors. The house passed away from our vision. We were not conscious of anything but the presence of the spirit and the cloud that was over us. We were wrapped in the cloud. A solemn awe pervaded us. We saw the cloud and felt the Spirit of the Lord. Then we heard a voice out of the *cloud saying*, "Prepare to receive the word of the Lord, for it is coming." At this we marveled greatly, but from that moment we knew that the word of the Lord was coming to Kirtland.[115]

Several months later, a carriage stopped at the Sidney Gilbert and Newel Whitney store in Kirtland. A pleasant and charismatic man got out of the carriage and walked into the store. "Newel K. Whitney," said the man enthusiastically as he offered his hand. Whitney replied, not knowing the man, "I could not call you by name as you have me." "I am Joseph the Prophet. You've prayed me here; now what do you want of me?" The astonished Whitney invited the Prophet Joseph, his wife Emma, and the two other men who accompanied them to his home that was located across the street. The Prophet accepted the invitation and followed Mr. Whitney to his home where he introduced his wife to the company. Elizabeth welcomed them into her home, and before the conclusion of their meeting, she said to her husband, "This [is] the fulfillment of the vision we had seen of a cloud, as of glory, resting upon our house."[116]

When the Prophet Joseph was asked in an interview with President Martin Van Buren what differed in the Mormon religion from all the others, Joseph replied that the Latter-day Saints differ "in mode of baptism, and the gift of the Holy Ghost by the laying on of hands."[117] Joseph Smith taught that only those persons who have received proper authority from God are permitted to perform baptism and bestow the gift of the Holy Ghost upon a person. "You might as well baptize a bag of sand as a man," stated the Prophet, "if not done in view of the remission of sins and getting of the Holy Ghost. Baptism by water is but half a baptism, and is good for nothing without the other half—that is, the baptism of the Holy Ghost."[118]

Asa Wild, a Methodist from West Fairlee, Vermont, was another visionary who published a manifestation similar to Stearns's mentioned previously. The Lord appeared to Wild and informed him that all denominations had become corrupt and that a restoration of Christ's Church would occur in the near future. This account was first published in the *Mohawk Herald* in Amsterdam, New York, on October 1, 1823, just ten days following Moroni's first appearance to Joseph Smith. E. B. Grandin and

Pomeroy Tucker published Wild's account in the Wayne Sentinel, also printed in Amsterdam, on October 22, 1823. Wild recorded,

> The Lord in his boundless goodness was pleased to communicate the following Revelation, having in the first place presented me with a very glorious Vision . . . It seemed as if my mind though active in its very nature, had lost all its activity, and was struck motionless, as well as into nothing, before the awful and glorious majesty of the Great Jehovah. He then spake to the following purport; and in such a manner as I could not describe if I should attempt. He told me that . . . *every denomination of professing Christians had become extremely corrupt*; many of which had never had any true faith at all; but are guided only by depraved reason, refusing the teaching of that Spirit which indited the scriptures, and which alone can teach us the true meaning of the same; even as the diamond alone can cut its fellow. *He told me further, that he had raised up, and was now raising up, that class of persons signified by the Angel mentioned by the Revelator* [Revelation 14:6–7], *which flew in the midst of heaven; having the everlasting gospel to preach; that these persons are in an inferior class, and small learning; that they will be rejected by every denomination as a body; but soon, God will open their way, by miracles, judgments, etc; that they will have higher authority, greater power, superior inspiration, and a greater degree of holiness, than was ever experienced before; inasmuch as this is far the most glorious dispensation of divine grace and glory.*[119]

Note that the Lord informed Wild not only of an imminent Restoration, but that the Restoration would be accompanied by "miracles" and "great power," which is the essence of this book! As far as we know, Wild never came in contact with Joseph Smith and was never baptized into the Church, which makes this account, as well as others mentioned in chapters 1 and 2, more remarkable.

Jesus Christ told Norris Stearns and Asa Wild that all existing churches were corrupt and that in the near future, the angel with the "Everlasting Gospel" would "fly in the midst of heaven" and would instigate a great work. John the Revelator saw the angel with the "Everlasting Gospel" in vision and subsequently

Nineteenth century rendition of the angel flying in the midst of heaven with a book containing the everlasting gospel recorded the following: "And I saw another angel fly in the midst of heaven, having the everlasting gospel to preach unto them that dwell on the earth, and to every nation, and kindred, and tongue, and people" (Revelation 14:6). Today, a statue of an angel can be seen standing atop many LDS temples holding a trumpet to his mouth. The trumpet symbolizes the preaching of the gospel to every nation, kindred, tongue, and people. On November 3, 1831, the Lord revealed to Joseph in vision that the angel referred to in Revelation 14 had come. "I have sent forth mine angel," revealed the Lord, "flying through the midst of heaven, having the everlasting gospel, who hath appeared unto some and hath committed it unto man, who shall appear unto many that dwell on the earth. And this gospel shall be preached unto every nation, and kindred, and tongue, and people" (D&C 133:36–37). One year earlier, the Lord told Joseph that Moroni came "to reveal the Book of Mormon, containing the fullness of *my everlasting gospel*" (D&C 27:5; emphasis added). In 1817, biblical scholar William Cuninghame, in commenting on Revelation 14:6, observed that it is "remarkable that this angel goes forth, not preaching by word of mouth only, but having the everlasting Gospel, (the book of the Gospel), the scriptures of truth, *in his hand*."[120] John Taylor, who as a child saw a vision of an angel flying in the heavens with a trumpet to his mouth (see chapter 3), described the everlasting gospel as follows:

John Taylor

> The everlasting gospel made known in the last days is nothing more or less than the ancient religion restored. It is the commencement of the "restitution of all things, spoken of by all the holy prophets since the world was." It is the bringing back of ancient, eternal principles, whereby men can know God as they knew him formerly; not a vague fantasy, not a simple form,

> but a living reality. Its doctrines, its ordinances, its principles, its priesthood are from above, revealed from the heavens, and yet strictly in conformity with all former revelations . . . It is adapted to the wants of the human family, to the world morally, socially, religiously and politically. It is not a sickly, sentimental, effeminate plaything; not a ghostly, spiritual, sing-song, ethereal dream, but a living, sober, matter-of-fact reality adapted to body and spirit, to earth and heaven, to time and eternity. It enters into all the ramifications of life. It does not adapt itself to the philosophy, politics, creeds, and opinions of men, but fashions them in its divine mold. It . . . lifts all that are in the world, who will be subject to its precepts . . . It searches all truth, and grasps at all intelligence. It is the revealed living and abiding will of God to man; a connection between the heavens and the earth. It is nature, philosophy, heavens and earth, time and eternity united. It is the philosophy of the heavens and the earth, of God, and angels, and saints.[121]

Conclusion

What can we conclude from the manifestations cited in this, as well as in the previous chapter? Were they the product of Satan's attempts to imitate the miracles of the Restoration of Christ's Church? Was Satan attempting to drown out the claims of Joseph Smith with noise, making him just another crazy religious fanatic claiming visionary experiences and trying to establish his own church? Or were these visionary experiences God's way of preparing the world for the Restoration of His Church by gradually enlightening the minds of men to the reality of angels, prophets, and revelation? "Unfortunately," explained Latter-day Saint scholar Richard Bushman, "we have no way to judge the authenticity of these visionary accounts: Some present fabulous, cumbersome stories that sound like the fantasies of troubled souls, straining one's credulity. Others . . . may have sobered readers and turned them to God . . . Inspired or not . . . the writings of . . . visionaries dispel the idea that revelations were unknown until the First Vision opened the heavens in 1820."[122]

After reviewing numerous accounts and statements in chapters 1 and 2, we learn that the claims of Joseph Smith were not as crazy and unprecedented as his critics have made them appear. Latter-day Saints teach of an apostasy, the necessity of a restoration, and that God and Christ are two separate individuals. All of these doctrines are supported in the aforementioned visionary accounts and statements, many of which were recorded and published by individuals not familiar with Joseph Smith and the Mormons.

We may also conclude that if God wanted to prepare the world—and especially a particular region—for the Restoration of His Church, then the way to accomplish that would be to open the minds of those people to accept angels, prophets, visions, and even evil spirits. One non-LDS scholar, Robert Remini, in discussing the inhabitants of the early American republic wrote, "These people believed in devils and witches as well as angels and divine messengers. And nothing in their occult practices was regarded as contrary to accepted Christian values or beliefs. It was a generation of seekers in search of faith by which they could govern their lives to the satisfaction of the Almighty."[123]

Despite all the arguments that can be posited regarding the manifestations presented in chapters 1 and 2, many valuable insights and themes emerge: (1) The heavens are not sealed and revelation did not cease, as many Christian denominations teach today. Revelation was as much a part of their world as it was to the ancient Israelites. (2) God the Father and Jesus Christ appeared numerous times as separate individuals with bodies like a man's. (3) Satan and evil spirits are real and often appear either in bodily form or as an unseen force to counter manifestations and revelations from heaven. (4) A restoration of Christ's Church was necessary according to scholars of various Christian denominations in past centuries. This belief prepared many to accept the restored gospel when it was presented to them. (5) Joseph Smith was not alone in claiming manifestations that taught of a restoration (see the map of visionaries in the northeastern states). (6) Heavenly manifestations often motivate individuals to do much good in their families and communities.

In short, the outpouring of spiritual manifestations in the eighteenth and early nineteenth centuries prepared individuals, families, and communities to accept the Restoration of Christ's Church. At minimum, the visionary and restoration culture of Joseph Smith's generation (and the previous generation) caused people to question some of the false traditions of their fathers and to reconsider their devotion to the Christ of the New Testament rather than the Christ of the creeds.

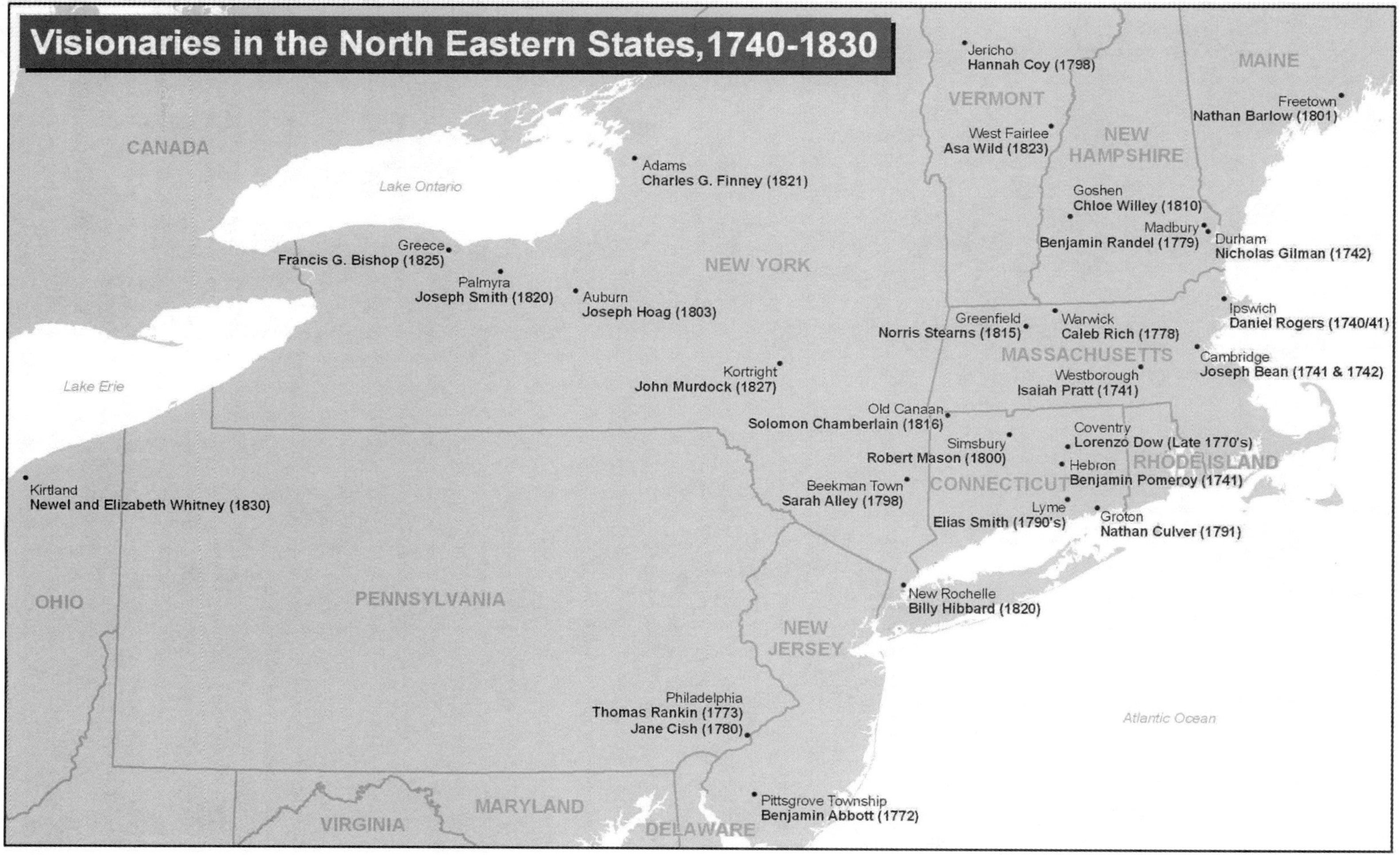
Visionaries in the North Eastern States, 1740-1830
Jericho
Hannah Coy (1798)
MAINE
VERMONT
Freetown
Nathan Barlow (1801)
West Fairlee
Asa Wild (1823)
NEW HAMPSHIRE
CANADA
Adams
Charles G. Finney (1821)
Lake Ontario
Goshen
Chloe Willey (1810)
Madbury
Benjamin Randel (1779)
Durham
Nicholas Gilman (1742)
Greece
Francis G. Bishop (1825)
NEW YORK
Palmyra
Joseph Smith (1820)
Auburn
Joseph Hoag (1803)
Ipswich
Daniel Rogers (1740/41)
Greenfield
Norris Stearns (1815)
Warwick
Caleb Rich (1778)
MASSACHUSETTS
Cambridge
Joseph Bean (1741 & 1742)
Westborough
Isaiah Pratt (1741)
Kortright
John Murdock (1827)
Lake Erie
Old Canaan
Solomon Chamberlain (1816)
Coventry
Lorenzo Dow (Late 1770's)
Simsbury
Robert Mason (1800)
Hebron
Benjamin Pomeroy (1741)
RHODE ISLAND
Kirtland
Newel and Elizabeth Whitney (1830)
Beekman Town
Sarah Alley (1798)
CONNECTICUT
Lyme
Elias Smith (1790's)
Groton
Nathan Culver (1791)
OHIO
PENNSYLVANIA
New Rochelle
Billy Hibbard (1820)
NEW JERSEY
Philadelphia
Thomas Rankin (1773)
Jane Cish (1780)
Atlantic Ocean
Pittsgrove Township
Benjamin Abbott (1772)
MARYLAND
VIRGINIA
DELAWARE

Chapter Three

Ancient Prophets and the Restoration

Joseph Smith claimed to have received many visitations of God's ancient prophets from Moroni's appearance to him on September 21, 1823, until he died in June 1844. In 1833, the Prophet Joseph Smith told Joseph B. Noble, while conversing about the Book of Mormon, that "voices of the angels had become so familiar that he knew their names before he saw them."[124] Many of these angels were ancient prophets who frequently appeared to assist Joseph Smith in restoring Christ's Church. Contained in this chapter are several accounts describing the appearances of several prophets from the ancient world. These accounts show that individuals who had previously lived on the earth assisted Joseph Smith and his associates a great deal in restoring Christ's Church.

The Prophet Moroni in the Restoration

Latter-day Saint historians are aware of approximately twenty occasions when the Prophet Joseph conversed with Moroni.[125] In addition, Moroni appeared to several other individuals (presented in this chapter and the next). All but one of these visits to Joseph occurred sometime between September 21, 1823, and June 25, 1829.[126] Moroni was present each time the plates were given to or taken from the Prophet Joseph, or each time the plates were shown to any individual other than the Eight Witnesses. Why, of all people, was Moroni called to prepare Joseph Smith for the Restoration? Elder Orson Hyde opined on this question in a discourse delivered on Independence Day in 1854.

> It was . . . that . . . angel of God [Moroni] that appeared unto Joseph Smith, and revealed to him the history of the early inhabitants of this country, whose mounds, bones and remains of towns, cities and fortifications speak from the dust in the ears of the living with the voice of undeniable truth. This same angel presides over the destinies of America, and feels a lively interest in all our doings. He was in the camp of [George] Washington; and, by an invisible hand, led on our fathers to conquest and victory; and all this to open and prepare the way for the Church and kingdom of God to be established on the western hemisphere, for the redemption of Israel and the salvation of the world.
>
> This same angel was with Columbus, and gave him deep impressions, by dreams and by visions, respecting this New World. . . . and the angel of God helped him—was with him on the stormy deep, calmed and troubled elements, and guided his frail vessel to the desired haven. Under the guardianship of this same angel, or Prince of America, have the United States grown, increased, and flourished, like the sturdy oak by the rivers of water.[127]

The idea that Moroni is the "Prince of America" and the guardian of the new nation is intriguing, especially in light of an ancient text dating to the first century AD, in which Pope Clement I (ca. AD 88–97) wrote, "*For every nation has an angel, to whom God has committed the government of that nation*. . . . The Most High God, who alone holds the power of all things, has divided all the nations of the earth into seventy-two parts, and over these He *hath appointed angels as princes*."[128] According to Elder Hyde, it was Moroni, the Prince of America, whom God appointed to be the guardian of this nation. In addition, the Doctrine and Covenants reveals that the Lord committed to Moroni "the keys of the record of the stick of Ephraim" (27:5), which explains why Moroni was the person who repeatedly appeared to Joseph Smith.

Preparing Joseph in the Early Years

"Moroni, in the beginning," stated George Q. Cannon, "came and ministered and talked to [Joseph] from time to time, and he had vision after vision in order that his mind might be fully saturated with knowledge of the things of God, and that he might comprehend the great and holy calling that God has bestowed upon him."[129] The first of these visions occurred on September 21, 1823, three and one-half years after Joseph's First Vision wherein he was told that "the fullness of the gospel should at some future time be made known unto [you]."[130] Since Joseph had not heard anything in over three years, he felt that the silence from heaven was the result of unworthiness.[131] As he prayed for forgiveness, a sudden burst of light entered his room and a heavenly personage stood before him.

> While I was praying unto God . . . a sudden light like that of day, only of a far purer and more glorious appearance, and brightness burst into the room, indeed the first sight was as though the house was filled with consuming fire; the appearance produced a shock that affected the whole body; in a moment a personage stood before me surrounded with a glory yet greater than that with which I was already surrounded. This messenger proclaimed himself to be an angel of God sent to bring the joyful tidings, that the covenant which God made with ancient Israel was at hand to be fulfilled, that the preparatory work for the second coming of the Messiah was speedily to commence; that the time was at hand for the gospel, in all its fullness to be preached in power, unto all nations that a people might be prepared for the millennial reign. I was informed that I was chosen to be an instrument in the hands of God to bring about some of his purposes in this glorious dispensation.[132]

Joseph recorded elsewhere that Moroni was the "common size of men in this age" and that his "garment was perfectly white, and had the appearance of being without seam."[133] Katharine Smith, sister of the Prophet, recalled that Joseph told her that "[Moroni] was dressed in white raiment, of whiteness beyond anything Joseph had ever seen in his life, and had a girdle about his waist."[134]

Moroni proceeded to inform Joseph about an ancient record secured in a hill nearly three miles from the Smith home. Moroni explained that the record contained a sacred history of remnants of the ancient Israelites, who were commanded to leave Jerusalem in the latter part of the seventh century and travel to the Americas. Joseph also learned that if he remained faithful, Moroni would deliver the record to him to translate. Following Moroni's descriptions of the Nephite people, a vision was opened to Joseph wherein he saw "the aboriginal inhabitants of this country, and [was] shown who they were, and from whence they came; a brief sketch of their origin, progress, civilization, laws, governments, of their righteousness and iniquity, and the blessings of God being finally withdrawn from them as a people was made known unto me." Joseph was again told "where there was deposited some plates on which were engraven an abridgement of the records of the ancient prophets that had existed on this continent."[135]

Moroni then showed Joseph another vision of "the place where the plates were deposited." He recorded that the vision was so clear and distinct that he recognized the place upon seeing it in person.[136] Joseph also learned that there were additional objects buried with the plates: "two stones in silver bows" known as the Urim and Thummim[137] and a breastplate on which the stones were attached. Moroni then told Joseph a third time that he would have the "privilege, if obedient to the commandments of the Lord, to obtain, and translate the same [the plates] by the means of the Urim and Thummim, which were deposited for that purpose with the record."[138]

After these visions of ancient America, Moroni quoted biblical passages to Joseph concerning the temple (Isaiah 2:1–4), the Book of Mormon (Isaiah 29:11–14), the gathering of Israel (Isaiah 43:6; Jeremiah 31:8–9), missionary work (Jeremiah 16:16), visions and dreams (Joel 2:28–32), the last days (Isaiah 11 Malachi 4:1–6), and the Second Coming (Malachi 3:1–3).[139] Following this instruction, Joseph recorded seeing "the light in the room . . . gather immediately around the person of him who had been speaking to me, and it continued to do so, until the room was again left dark, except just around me, when instantly I saw, as it were, a conduit open right up into heaven, and he ascended until he entirely disappeared, and the room was left as it had been before this heavenly light had made its appearance." Soon after the light faded, Joseph fell into a state of deep meditation where he "lay musing on the singularity of the scene and marveling greatly." Joseph received two subsequent visits from the angel on this same night.[140]

Lucy Mack Smith commented on frequent family conversations conducted shortly after Moroni's first appearances that provide further insight into what Joseph saw in vision: "During our evening conversations, Joseph would occasionally . . . describe the ancient inhabitants of this continent, their dress, mode of traveling, and the animals upon which they rode; their cities, their buildings, with every particular; their mode of warfare; and also their religious worship. This he would do with as much ease, seemingly, as if he had spent his whole life among them."[141]

The morning after his first encounter with Moroni, Joseph arose and attended to the usual "labors of the day" but was unproductive because of fatigue from lack of sleep. Noticing his condition, Joseph's father admonished him to go back to the house and rest. Before Joseph arrived at the house Moroni appeared to him for the fourth time.

> I started with the intention of going to the house, but in attempting to cross the fence out of the field where we were, my strength entirely failed me and I fell helpless on the ground and for a time was quite unconscious of anything. The first thing that I can recollect was a voice speaking unto me calling me by name. I looked up and beheld the same messenger standing over my head surrounded by light as before. He then again related unto me all that he had related to me the previous night, and commanded me to go to my father and tell him of the vision and commandments which I had received. I obeyed. I returned back to my father in the field and rehearsed the whole matter to him. He replied to

> me, that it was of God, and to go and do as commanded by the messenger. I left the field and went to the place where the messenger had told me the plates were deposited, and owing to the distinctness of the vision which I had had concerning it, I knew the place the instant that I arrived there.[142]

Joseph recorded that the plates were buried "on the west side of this hill not far from the top." As he approached the location, Joseph discovered a large rock that was "thick and rounding in the middle on the upper side, and thinner towards the edges, so that the middle part of it was visible above the ground, but the edge all round was covered with earth." Joseph dug around the rock and raised it up with a small log acting as a lever. As Joseph looked under the rock, he reported seeing the "plates, the Urim and Thummim, and the Breastplate." Joseph also described the box in which the plates were placed as being "formed by laying stones together in some kind of cement; in the bottom of the box were laid two stones crossways of the box, and on these stones lay the plates and the other things with them."[143] When Joseph reached into the box he felt a shock that prevented him from obtaining the plates. In other accounts we learn that he was actually lifted up off the ground by an "unseen power"[144] and "hurled back"[145] away from where the plates were buried. Oliver Cowdery provided details of Joseph's reaction.

> He desisted for an instant, and then made another attempt, but was more sensibly shocked than before. . . . He therefore made the third attempt with an increased exertion, when his strength failed him more than at either of the former times, and without premeditating he exclaimed, "Why can I not obtain this book?" "Because you have not kept the commandments of the Lord," answered a voice, within a seeming short distance. He looked, and to his astonishment, there stood the angel who had previously given him the directions concerning this matter. In an instant, all the former instructions, the great intelligence concerning Israel and the last days, were brought to his mind: he thought of the time when his heart was fervently engaged in prayer to the Lord, when his spirit was contrite, and when his holy messenger from the skies unfolded the wonderful things connected with this

> record. He had come, to be sure, and found the word of the angel fulfilled concerning the reality of the record, but he had failed to remember the great end for which they had been kept, and in consequence could not have power to take them into his possession and bear them away.[146]

Moroni immediately opened a vision to Joseph where he was shown Satan and his "innumerable train of associates" to help him learn to differentiate between the power of God and the power of Satan. Moroni subsequently taught Joseph that "whatever entices and leads to good and to do good, is of God, and whatever does not is of that wicked one: It is he that fills the hearts of men with evil, to walk in darkness and blaspheme God; and you may learn from henceforth, that his ways are to destruction, but the way of holiness is peace and rest. You now see why you could not obtain this record."[147] Moroni informed Joseph that he would receive a sign in the near future regarding these prophecies and that some would also seek to destroy his reputation with falsehoods. Joseph's mother recalled that "the angel told him, that the time had not yet come for the plates to be brought forth to the world; that he could not take them from the place wherein they were deposited until he had learned to keep the commandments of God—not only till he was willing but able to do it."[148]

Lucy Smith also recorded that Joseph had received the plates on September 22, 1824; however, due to carelessness, the plates were immediately taken from him.

> Joseph again visited the place where he found the plates the year previous . . . and uncovering the plates, he put forth his hand and took them up, but, as he was taking them hence, the unhappy thought darted through his mind that probably there was something else in the box besides the plates, which would be of some pecuniary advantage to him. So, in the moment of excitement, he laid them down very carefully, for the purpose of covering the box, lest someone might happen to pass that way and get whatever there might be remaining in it. After covering it, he turned round to take the Record again, but behold it was gone,

and where he knew not, neither did he know the means by which it had been taken from him.

At this, as a natural consequence, he was much alarmed. He kneeled down and asked the Lord why the Record had been taken from him; upon which the angel of the Lord appeared to him, and told him that he had not done as he had been commanded, for in a former revelation he had been commanded not to lay the plates down, or put them for a moment out of his hands, until he got into the house and deposited them in a chest or trunk, having a good lock and key, and, contrary to this, he had laid them down with the view of securing some fancied or imaginary treasure that remained. In the moment of excitement, Joseph was overcome by the powers of darkness, and forgot the injunction that was laid upon him.[149]

Moroni instructed Joseph to return each year to Cumorah on September 22 where he would receive "instruction and intelligence . . . respecting what the Lord was going to do, and how and in what manner his kingdom was to be conducted in the last days."[150]

Shortly after he married Emma Hale, Joseph was severely reprimanded by Moroni while on a business errand to Manchester for his father. Joseph Sr. and Lucy were expecting Joseph to return around six o'clock in the evening but grew worried when he did not return until nine o'clock. Lucy related the conversation they had with Joseph following his return.

On coming in he threw himself into a chair, apparently much exhausted. My husband did not observe his appearance and immediately exclaimed, "Joseph, why are you so late? Has anything happened to you? We have been much distressed about you these three hours." As Joseph made no answer he continued his interrogations, until, finally, I said, "Now, father, let him rest a moment—don't trouble him now—you see he is home safe and he is very tired, so pray wait a little."

The fact was I had learned to be a little cautious about matters with regard to Joseph, for I was accustomed to see him look as he did on that occasion and I could not easily mistake the cause thereof. Presently he smiled and said in a calm tone, "I have taken the severest chastisement that I have ever had in my life."

My husband, supposing that it was from some of the

> neighbors, was quite angry and observed, "I would like to know what business anybody has to find fault with you!" "Stop, father, stop," said Joseph, "it was the angel of the Lord. As I passed by the hill of Cumorah, where the plates are, the angel met me and said that I had not been engaged enough in the work of the Lord; that the time had come for the record to be brought forth; and that I must be up and doing and set myself about the things which God had commanded me to do. But, father, give yourself no uneasiness concerning the reprimand which I have received, for I now know the course that I am to pursue, so all will be well."[151]

Joseph Receives the Plates

On September 22, 1827, shortly following Joseph's arrival to the hill, Moroni appeared and instructed him as he had done for four consecutive years. Moroni gave Joseph the plates and told him that if he were to be negligent with them and let them "go carelessly," that he would be "cut off"; however, if he were to use all of his "endeavors to preserve them . . . they should be protected."[152] Lucy Smith reported that Joseph, after receiving the plates, was told, "you will have to be watchful and faithful . . . or you will be overpowered by wicked men; for they will lay every plan and scheme that is possible to get [the plates] away from you, and if you do not take heed continually, they will succeed. . . . Beware, and look well to your ways, and you shall have power to retain it, until the time for it to be translated."[153] For the next several months, Joseph spent a great deal of time and energy protecting the plates from mobs, neighbors, and acquaintances who frequently attempted to get to them.

With the assistance of Martin Harris, Joseph began translating the plates in December 1827, and by June 1828 they had translated 116 pages. Shortly after, Moroni punished Joseph and Martin because the latter had taken the manuscript home and subsequently lost it.[154] Moroni took the plates and the Urim and Thummim from Joseph and said, "If you are very humble and penitent, it may be you will receive them again; if so, it will be on the twenty-second of next September [1828]."[155] Moroni appeared to Joseph several times prior to September 22, 1828, bringing the Urim and Thummim for the purpose of delivering revelations to him via them.[156]

When Joseph received the plates and the Urim and Thummim on September 22, 1828, Moroni told him that Martin Harris was no longer permitted to assist in the translation of the plates but that the Lord would send a new scribe. In the meantime, Joseph proceeded in the translation with his wife, Emma, serving as his scribe;[157] although, very little was accomplished between September 1828 and April 1829 due to financial struggles and other setbacks.

In the spring of 1829, Lyman Cowdery was hired to teach at the school in Manchester, New York, that was located near the Smith home. Lyman was unable to accept the position and suggested that his brother Oliver be hired in his place. In March 1829, Oliver arrived in Manchester where he was invited to live in the Smith home while teaching. Within a few weeks Oliver learned about Joseph's heavenly manifestations and the plates and felt that the information given him was true. He soon left Manchester for Harmony, Pennsylvania, where Joseph and Emma were living.[158] Oliver arrived in Harmony on April 5, met the Prophet Joseph, and expressed his interest in acting as scribe in the translation project. Joseph accepted Oliver's offer and they began translating on April 7, 1829. By June 25, 1829 the translation was complete.

Symbolic Significance of Moroni's Visits

Moroni's role in the Restoration was paramount. His appearances were not only pragmatic in preparing Joseph for his prophetic calling, but many of them were highly symbolic. When Joseph prayed to receive further revelation on September 21, 1823, Moroni appeared and taught him concerning the ancient prophecies and instructed him on the last days. But why did Moroni appear on this particular night? What was so special about this day? Perhaps Moroni visited Joseph on September 21, 1823, because this day was a holy day to the ancient Israelites and

Jews. Specifically, this was day two of the seven-day Sukkoth festival, also known as the Feast of Tabernacles or Feast of Booths.[159] God commanded the Israelites to set aside this time every year for remembering their ancestors who wandered in the wilderness for forty years (see Leviticus 23:34; Deuteronomy 16:13).[160] Moreover, Sukkoth carried symbolic significance for the Restoration of God's kingdom in the last days.

During Sukkoth the priests led prayers at the temple. These prayers were accompanied by a ceremony of drawing water from the pool of Siloam (Jerusalem's water source) that was subsequently poured onto the altar at the temple. Both the prayers and this water libation ceremony were performed in supplication to God requesting that He bless them with rain. Anyone who has spent a summer in Israel knows that by the fall festivals, the land is extremely arid and rain is a necessity. The Sukkoth festival, including the water ceremonies and the prayers for rain, carried deep spiritual symbolism. "Rain," according to one non-LDS scholar, "was a prominent feature in the celebration of the Feast of Sukkoth. . . . The Rain represented the Holy Spirit and the water drawing pointed to that day when, according to the prophet Joel, God would rain His Spirit upon all flesh (Joel 2:28–29)."[161] Notice that Moroni quoted Joel 2:28–32 to Joseph on this night. This scholar continues,

> Sukkoth was given by God to teach us of the Messianic era . . . when the earth will experience the greatest outpouring of God's Spirit. . . . The rain is a type of the *Holy Spirit being poured out upon all flesh* (Acts: 2:1–8, 14–21; Joel 2:23, 28–29) . . . . Rain also speaks *of revival, restoration,* and returning to God and trusting in Him. . . . The great rain or outpouring of God's Holy Spirit will come when the believers in the Messiah will earnestly pray to God that it be done. God has already declared that he would pour out *His Holy Spirit during the seventh month* [Tishrei/September] . . . This outpouring will touch every nation, both Jew and non-Jew.[162]

The rabbis and temple priests studied the ancient prophecies concerning the last days on Sukkoth. Similarly, on this night, Moroni taught Joseph Smith the biblical prophecies concerning the last days. Joseph also prayed, moments prior to the arrival of Moroni, that he would receive further revelation, as he had heard nothing since his 1820 visitation. As previously described, praying for further prophecy and revelation was a major practice of God's covenant people during Sukkoth.

As discussed in the first two chapters, Christians from all denominations during Joseph Smith's generation believed that God would pour out his Spirit (and spiritual gifts) upon all flesh. Joseph Smith was specifically told this on Sukkoth during Moroni's first visit. Jesus also, during Sukkoth, taught, "If any man thirst, let him come unto me, and drink. He that believeth on me, as the scripture hath said, out of his belly shall flow rivers of living water" (John 7:37–38). "Living water" not only symbolizes revelation and the Holy Spirit, but also symbolizes the "nations of the earth."[163] Joseph clearly understood, following Moroni's visits on September 21, 1823, that he was called to be a prophet in the last days and would translate a book of scripture containing the Everlasting Gospel to go forth to all "nations of the earth."

As previously mentioned, Moroni appeared to Joseph two additional times the following day. Moroni informed Joseph that he would return every year for the next four years on September 22 to give him further instruction. Note that each of these days fell on the autumn equinox,[164] one of two days a year when continual light emanates from the sun or the moon, and when the sun rises exactly in the east. This is symbolic because continual light represents continual revelation, a characteristic of the last days and the Restoration. East is a symbol for heaven and the dwelling place of God, and it will be the Messiah who will come from the east when he returns.[165]

The most significant of these September 22 visits occurred in 1827. This date is well known among Latter-day Saints as the day when Joseph Smith received the plates. Not only did September 22, 1827, fall on the autumn equinox, but it also happened to be

Ancient Jewish temple priest blowing a ram's horn,
courtesy of Dan McClellan

one of the Israelite high holy days, Rosh Hashanah,[166] also known as the Feast of Trumpets. On this ancient holy day, the trumpet (ram's horn or "shofar") is sounded in celebration of the future gathering of Israel, the rebuilding of the temple, and the coming of the Messiah. The trumpet blast on Rosh Hashanah symbolically "awakens" God's children from a "spiritual slumber," stated one non-LDS source (see Isaiah 42:11; 44:23; Jeremiah 31:7; 1 Corinthians 15:46).[167] That the Feast of Trumpets would be the day appointed by God for Joseph to receive the gold plates seems fitting. Also note that after Moroni took the plates from Joseph, due to Martin Harris losing the 116-page manuscript, he was promised that if he repented and remained faithful, the plates would be returned to him on September 22, 1828,[168] the day of autumn equinox and the eve of the Sukkoth festival.

Concerning these ancient connections, note Alma's thought that "all things denote there is a God; yea, even the earth, and all things that are upon the face of it, yea, and its motion, yea, and also all the planets which move in their regular form do witness that there is a Supreme Creator" (Alma 30:44). All God's creations move at his command and testify of his existence. This is due to the incredible order in which they were created. Furthermore, we read in Colossians 2:16–17 that the Israelite feasts and holy days were established by God to prophesy of future events and are "a shadow of things to come."

Moroni Appears to Other Individuals

Moroni appeared to several individuals other than Joseph Smith and the Three Witnesses to the Book of Mormon. John Taylor received many spiritual manifestations as a child while living in Milnthorpe, England. "Frequently when alone," recalled Taylor, "and sometimes in company I heard sweet soft melodious music, as if performed by angelic or supernatural beings."[169] When Taylor was a boy, somewhere between the ages of five and eleven, he "saw in vision an angel in the heavens, *holding a trumpet to his mouth, sounding a message to the nations.*"[170]

Robert Smith, friend of President Heber C. Kimball, related the occasion when Moroni appeared to President Kimball prior to his death. "At family prayers," reported Smith, "just a little while before his death, he remarked that the Angel Moroni had visited him the night before and had informed him that his work on this earth was finished and he would soon be taken."[171] Heber died the morning of June 22, 1868.

Moroni also visited Oliver Granger in 1830 while he contemplated joining the Church (see chapter 6), Lucy Harris in 1827 while in conflict with her husband Martin over the translation project (see chapter 4), Mary Whitmer in 1829 while she struggled with the work load caused by the translation project (see chapter 4), and Harrison Burgess in 1833 to testify of the Book of Mormon (see chapter 4).

Before continuing to the next section, it is worth noting that Moroni was not the only prophet to teach and assist Joseph Smith in his work with the translation of the plates; several other Book of Mormon prophets may have assisted Joseph as well. Wilford Woodruff explained that Joseph translated the plates "according to the dictation of Moroni, Nephi and Lehi, the angels of God who administered to him."[172] John Taylor also spoke of the assistance of Book of Mormon prophets in the early days of the Restoration: "when Joseph Smith was raised up as a Prophet of God, Mormon, Moroni, Nephi and others of the ancient Prophets who formerly lived on this Continent . . . came to him and communicated to him certain principles pertaining to the Gospel of the Son of God. Why? Because they held the keys of the various dispensations and conferred them upon him."[173] Brigham Young said that Alma was among those prophets who appeared to Joseph in the early days of the Restoration.[174]

At least two individuals recorded that a "Nephite" visited the Prophet Joseph. One of these individuals was Helen M. Whitney: "In another letter I find an interesting item concerning the Prophet Joseph's receiving a visit from one of the Nephites, who told him he had been through England, Ireland and that the work of the Lord would be short and powerful in those places. He also told him many things about this land (America), many of which have been fulfilled.[175] Heber C. Kimball's wife, Vilate, similarly explained that Joseph received "a visit from one of the Nephites" and that he became aware of things that would shortly transpire in America and in the British Isles.[176] We do not know the identity of this Nephite, but Helen and Vilate likely could have been referring to Moroni or one of the Three Nephites.

Perhaps many of these Book of Mormon prophets appeared to Joseph Smith to assist him at certain points in the translation process. It appears that Joseph translated the plates with a seer stone and Urim and Thummim (see chapter 5), but may have also received commentary directly from those who wrote portions of the Book of Mormon. As explained by Joseph's mother, the Smith family would often reserve evenings to hear Joseph describe at length the lifestyle and other details regarding the ancient Nephites. Joseph would have learned these things in vision, by ancient Nephite prophets, or both. It is no wonder that Joseph was able to translate the Book of Mormon as quickly as he did, since he had constant assistance from heaven.

Emeritus Professor of History at the University of Illinois at Chicago Robert V. Remini, a non-LDS scholar, was amazed by the rapid translation of the Book of Mormon: "What is truly remarkable—really miraculous—is the fact that this massive translation was completed in sixty working days by an uneducated but highly imaginative zealot steeped in the religious fervor of his age. As a writer, I find that feat absolutely incredible. Sixty days! Two months to produce a work running over six hundred pages and of such complexity and density. Unbelievable."[177] Concerning the impact of the Book of Mormon, Henry Wallace, vice president of the United States (1941–1945) and secretary of commerce under Presidents Roosevelt and Truman opined: "Of all the American books of the nineteenth century, it seems probable that the Book of Mormon was the most powerful. It reached perhaps only one percent of the United States, but it affected this one percent so powerfully and lastingly that all the people of the United States have been affected, especially by its contribution, in opening one of our great frontiers."[178] Another non-LDS scholar and well-known historian, Gordon Wood, suggested that the Book of Mormon was published at the perfect time for it to take hold in America.

> The Book of Mormon is an extraordinary work of popular imagination and one of the greatest documents in American cultural history. Its timing in 1830 was providential. It appeared at precisely the right moment in American history; much earlier or later and the Church might not have taken hold. The Book of Mormon would probably not have been published in the eighteenth century . . . And . . . if Mormonism had emerged later, after the consolidation of authority and the spread of science in the middle decades of the nineteenth century, it might have had problems of verifying its texts and revelations. But during the *early decades of the nineteenth century* the time was ideally suited for the establishment of the new faith.[179]

Completing the task of producing, in a span of approximately two and one-half months, a massive manuscript containing a complex narrative is impressive. To accomplish that, however, with as little educational training as the Prophet Joseph possessed, is phenomenal and smacks of divine assistance. That assistance, according to the Prophet and his closest associates, came by ancient prophets.

Regarding the Prophet's preparation to restore the Church and his seeming connection with the ancient world, Richard T. Hughes of Pepperdine University stated,

> When I. Woodbridge Riley claimed that Joseph's Book of Mormon embodied popular American themes . . . he missed the most important theme of all, and that was the cosmic rhythm of restoration and millennium that defined both the nation and most of the nation's new religions.
>
> In making this argument, I have no doubt come across as a reductionist with a vengeance, as the typical non-Mormon who wants to argue that "America created Joseph Smith." But in my view, there is far more to Joseph than this. . . . Joseph has a history

> that extends beyond the United States. That history, in my view, is preeminently the biblical saga, . . . For this is a cosmic history that shaped the Prophet in cosmic ways. But even as that cosmic, biblical history shaped the Prophet in cosmic ways, it did so in a profoundly American context. In this way, Joseph Smith emerges as the dialectical prophet, the man with one foot in American culture and the other in biblical culture, and the man who fused the two in a profound act of creative genius.[180]

Hughes undoubtedly does not believe that Joseph conversed with these ancient prophets in connection with the translation, as he attributed the Book of Mormon to the work of a "creative genius"; but it is worth noting that he linked Joseph Smith and Mormonism to the ancient world. Latter-day Saints believe that the translation of the plates and the Restoration was not the creative work of a genius but of several ancient prophets alongside a divinely called, latter-day prophet.

Biblical Prophets in the Restoration

While translating the portion of the plates that recounts Christ's visit to the inhabitants of the Americas and his instruction to them regarding baptism (3 Nephi 11), Joseph and Oliver Cowdery decided to pray for further knowledge on the issue. On May 15, 1829, Joseph and Oliver knelt in prayer near the Susquehanna River when John the Baptist appeared. Joseph related the experience:

> While we were thus employed, praying and calling upon the Lord, a messenger from heaven descended in a cloud of light, and having laid his hands upon us, he ordained us, saying: "Upon you my fellow servants, in the name of Messiah I confer the Priesthood of Aaron, which holds the keys of the ministering of angels, and of the Gospel of repentance, and of baptism by immersion for the remission of sins; and this shall never be taken again from the earth, until the sons of Levi do offer again an offering unto the Lord in righteousness." He said this Aaronic Priesthood had not the power of laying on hands for the gift of the Holy Ghost, but that this should be conferred on us hereafter; and he

> commanded us to go and be baptized, and gave us directions that I should baptize Oliver Cowdery, and afterwards that he should baptize me. Accordingly we went and were baptized. I baptized him first, and afterwards he baptized me, after which I laid my hands upon his head and ordained him to the Aaronic Priesthood, and afterwards he laid his hands on me and ordained me to the same Priesthood—for so we were commanded.
>
> The messenger who visited us on this occasion, and conferred this Priesthood upon us, said that his name was John, the same that is called John the Baptist in the New Testament, and that he acted under the direction of Peter, James and John who held the keys of the Priesthood of Melchizedek, which Priesthood he said would in due time be conferred on us.[181]

The authority to administer ordinances of God is fundamental to Latter-day Saints. The appearance of John the and the conferral of priesthood authority to Joseph Smith and Oliver Cowdery differentiate the Latter-day Saints from every other Christian group. "Do the Mormons baptize in the name of 'Joe' Smith?," asked the Prophet. "No, but if they did, it would be as valid as the baptism administered by the sectarian priests."[182] The Prophet Joseph later expounded on this doctrine: "We believe that no man can administer salvation through the gospel, to the souls of men, in the name of Jesus Christ, except he is authorized from God, by revelation, or by being ordained by someone whom God hath sent by revelation, as it is written by Paul . . . Hebrews, 5:4, 'And no man taketh this honor unto himself, but he that is called of God, as was Aaron.' And I would ask, how was Aaron called, but by revelation?"[183]

In late May or early June 1829, Peter, James, and John appeared to Joseph Smith and Oliver Cowdery and conferred upon them the Melchizedek Priesthood just as John the Baptist said they would. "I received the holy priesthood," stated Joseph Smith, "by the ministering of angels to administer the letter of the gospel. I received the high priesthood after the holy order of the son of the living God. I received the power [and the authority] to preach the gospel and administer in the ordinances [thereof].

The keys of the kingdom [were also] conferred upon me."[184]

Shortly following the establishment of the Church in April 1830, Joseph Smith and Sidney Rigdon were commanded by God to begin translating the Bible. This translation project intended to restore meaning that was lost over time, as well as add insight into the scriptures. Joseph understood fully that this work was a "branch of his calling."[185] It may have been during this translation process when several biblical prophets visited Joseph Smith. John Taylor stated that the Apostles Peter and John, as well as "others who lived on the Asiatic Continent," appeared to Joseph and "communicated to him certain principles pertaining to the Gospel of the Son of God."[186] Doctrine and Covenants 128:21 also reveals that he was taught by many "diverse angels from, Michael or Adam down to the present time, all declaring their dispensation, their rights, their keys, their honors, their majesty and glory, and the power of their priesthood; giving line upon line, precept upon precept; here a little, and there a little; giving us consolation by holding forth that which is to come."

As Joseph Smith and Sidney Rigdon were translating John 5:29 in the John Johnson home on February 16, 1832, a vision opened to them in which they saw the condition of heaven and God's dwelling place. They described seeing God the Father, Jesus Christ, "holy angels," and many ancient priests who held the "Melchizedek" Priesthood.[187] Joseph stated that this vision was a full body experience where he was "full of light" and that he "could see even out at the ends of [his] fingers and toes."[188] Philo Dibble was present when Joseph and Sidney saw the vision and related the experience as follows:

> The vision which is recorded in the book of Doctrine and Covenants was given at the house of "Father Johnson," in Hyrum, Ohio, and during the time that Joseph and Sidney were in the spirit and saw the heavens open, there were other men in the room, perhaps twelve, among whom I was one during a part of the time—probably two-thirds of the time—I saw the glory and felt the power, but did not see the vision. . . .

> Joseph would, at intervals, say: "What do I see?" as one might say while looking out the window and Beholding what all in the room could not see. Then he would relate what he had seen or what he was looking at. Then Sidney replied, "I see the same." Presently Sidney would say: "What do I see?" and would repeat what he had seen or was seeing, and Joseph would reply, "I see the same."
>
> This manner of conversation was repeated at short intervals to the end of the vision, and during the whole time not a word was spoken by any other person. Not a sound nor motion was made by anyone but Joseph and Sidney, and it seemed to me that they never moved a joint or limb during the time I was there, which I think was over an hour, and to the end of the vision.[189]

Johnson home, photo taken by Megan Hatch

Dibble described Joseph, who was wearing "black clothes," as appearing to "be dressed in an element of glorious white, and his face shone as if it were transparent, but I did not see the same glory attending Sidney. Joseph appeared as strong as a lion, but Sidney seemed as weak as water, and Joseph noticing his condition smiled and said, 'Brother Sidney is not as used to it as I am.' "[190] The Prophet also commented on this vision.

> Nothing could be more pleasing to the Saints upon the order of the Kingdom of the Lord, than the light which burst upon the world through the foregoing vision. Every law, every commandment, every promise, every truth, and every point touching the destiny of man, from Genesis to Revelation, where the purity of the Scriptures remain unsullied by the folly of men, go to show the perfection of the theory (of different degrees of glory in the future life) and witness the fact that the document is a transcript from the records of the eternal world. The sublimity of the ideas; the purity of the language; the scope for action; the continued duration for completion, in order that the heirs of salvation may confess the Lord and bow the knee; the rewards for faithfulness, and the punishments for sins, are so much beyond the narrow-mindedness of men, that every man is constrained to exclaim: "It came from God."[191]

Joseph and Sidney recorded only a small percentage of what they saw in the vision because the Prophet said, "I could explain a hundred fold more than I ever have of the glories of the kingdoms manifested to me in the vision, were I permitted, and were the people prepared to receive them."[192] Orson Pratt stated that Joseph and Sidney were commanded to record only "some of these things" that they saw and were "strictly commanded" not to record the rest of what they beheld "as the world was not worthy to receive them. Neither was the Church at that time prepared to receive a full knowledge concerning these things."[193] The current LDS edition of the Doctrine and Covenants reveals that "all the faithful may see the vision" that was shown to Joseph and Sidney if they are prepared to receive it, and also if they are worthy of such manifestations.[194] Speaking of this revelation and vision, Wilford Woodruff stated, "Before I saw Joseph I said I did not care how old he was, or how young he was; I did not care how he looked, whether his hair was long or short; the man that advanced that revelation was a prophet of God"[195]

Ancient prophets and Apostles also visited Joseph many times following the completion of the Bible translation. Martha C.

Cox, for example, recounted an occasion in Nauvoo when Joseph Smith spoke face to face with John the Revelator in the presence of Allen Stout, one of the Prophet's bodyguards.

> Allen Stout . . . used to come to live with us while he worked in the temple. . . . He was in Nauvoo a bodyguard to the Prophet, and when asked to tell something about the days of Nauvoo he would tell it, but he was not much of a talker unless asked to do so. He gave me much information about the early history of the Church because I asked him many questions. One day he said in answer to a statement that I thought it could not be possible for one to see a heavenly being, that I might see one without recognizing it as such—as happened once with him. I immediately became anxious to know all about it. He told me [he] was once walking with the Prophet on the west side of the Mississippi River on the road to Montrose, I think. They saw a man walking along a road leading in from the south and coming towards them. The Prophet told Allen to remain where he was while he stepped over to speak with this pedestrian. Allen turned his back towards them and for a time forgot the Prophet and became engaged with his own thought, while he stood whipping a low bush with the cane he carried. The hand of the Prophet upon his shoulder aroused him. The Prophet said, "We must return immediately to Nauvoo." They walked silently and rapidly. Allen became very sorrowful over his recreancy to his duty and could not refrain from weeping. The Prophet asked him why he wept. Allen confessed, "I am an insufficient bodyguard—criminally neglectful of your welfare. I allowed that man you met to speak with you without even being ready to defend if he attacked you. He could have killed you and made his escape without my knowing who he is, which way he went or what he even looks like. You will have to dispense with my services and take a guard on which you can depend. Your life is too precious to be trusted to my care." The Prophet then said, "That man would not harm me. You saw John the Revelator."[196]

On another occasion, Joseph gathered the presidency and the Apostles to administer and partake of the sacrament on the afternoon of Easter Sunday, April 3, 1836. Following the passing of the sacrament, the curtain near the pulpit was lowered, behind which Oliver Cowdery and the Prophet knelt in prayer. Heavenly messengers appeared and conferred upon them the "keys" pertaining to the priesthood of God. The Prophet Joseph recounted the event as follows:

> After this vision [of Christ] closed, the heavens were again opened unto us; and Moses appeared before us, and committed unto us the keys of the gathering of Israel from the four parts of the earth, and the leading of the ten tribes from the land of the north.
>
> After this, Elias appeared, and committed the dispensation of the gospel of Abraham, saying that in us and our seed all generations after us should be blessed. After this vision had closed, another great and glorious vision burst upon us; for Elijah the prophet, who was taken to heaven without tasting death, stood before us, and said:
>
> Behold, the time has fully come, which was spoken of by the mouth of Malachi—testifying that he [Elijah] should be sent, before the great and dreadful day of the Lord come—
>
> To turn the hearts of the fathers to the children, and the children to the fathers, lest the whole earth be smitten with a curse—
>
> Therefore, the keys of this dispensation are committed into your hands; and by this ye may know that the great and dreadful day of the Lord is near, even at the doors.[197]

In July 1839, Joseph Smith reported seeing a vision of Adam in the valley of Adam-ondi-Ahman surrounded by his posterity. Adam called each one of them forth and blessed them. Joseph also saw "The Lord appear in their midst."[198] The Prophet seemed, according to John Taylor, "to be as familiar with these [prophets] as we are with one another."[199] This comment corresponds with the account that relates the occasion when Joseph, in casual conversation, compared the looks of his oldest brother Alvin, who had already passed away, to Adam and Seth: "[Alvin] was a very handsome man, surpassed by none other but Adam and Seth."[200] Joseph also described Adam as "such a perfect man, great and stout, that he never stumbled or fell a joint to the ground."[201] Joseph told Elizabeth Tyler that he had seen Adam on several occasions when he learned that Elizabeth Tyler had also seen Adam in vision. Elizabeth's son Daniel related the incident.

> A short time prior to his [Joseph's] arrival at my father's house, my mother, Elizabeth Comins Tyler, had a remarkable vision. Lest it might be attributed to the evil one, she related it to no person, except my father, Andrew Tyler, until the Prophet arrived, on his way to Canada, I think. She saw a man sitting upon a white cloud, clothed in white from head to foot. He had a peculiar cap, different from any she had ever seen, with a white robe, underclothing, and moccasins. It was revealed to her that this person was Michael [Adam], the Archangel. The Prophet informed her that she had had a true vision. He had seen the same angel several times. It was Michael, the Archangel.[202]

Zebedee Coltrin, future president in the Council of the Seventy, recorded a vision that he, along with the Prophet and Oliver Cowdery, saw of Adam and Eve. This vision took place on April 18, 1834, in Kirtland, Ohio:

> After returning from a mission to Kirtland, I met Brother Joseph, who asked me if I did not wish to go with him to a conference at New Portage, Ohio. The party consisted of Presidents Joseph Smith, Sidney Rigdon, Oliver Cowdery and me. Next morning at New Portage, I noticed that Joseph seemed to have a far off look in his eyes, or was looking at a distance. Presently he stepped between Brother Cowdery and me, and taking us by the arm said, "Let's take a walk." We went to a place where there was some beautiful grass, and grapevines and swamp birch interlaced. President Joseph Smith then said, "Let us pray." We all three prayed in turn—Joseph, Oliver and me. Brother Joseph then said, "Now brethren, we will see some visions." Joseph lay down on the ground on his back and stretched out his arms, and we laid on them. The heavens gradually opened, and we saw a golden throne, on a circular foundation, and on the throne sat a man and a woman, having white hair and clothed in white garments. Their heads were white as snow, and their faces shone with immortal youth. They were the two most beautiful and perfect specimens of mankind I ever saw. Joseph said, "They are our first parents, Adam and Eve." Adam was a large broad shouldered man, and Eve, as a woman, was as large in proportion.[203]

During a Kirtland Temple dedicatory session on March 27, 1836, the Prophet Joseph called the brethren together and proceeded to bestow upon them temple blessings. Heber C. Kimball, who was present, explained that the Apostle John appeared in their midst.

> When the Prophet Joseph had finished the endowments of the First Presidency, the Twelve and the Presiding Bishops, the First Presidency proceeded to lay hands upon each one of them to seal and confirm the anointing; and at the close of each blessing the whole of the quorums responded to it with a loud shout of Hosanna . . . While these things were being attended to the beloved disciple John was seen in our midst by the Prophet Joseph, Oliver Cowdery and others.[204]

During this same dedicatory session, at least six individuals reported that a heavenly messenger appeared and sat down in the vacant seat between Joseph Smith Sr. and Fredrick G. Williams. "President Frederick G. Williams," recorded the Prophet Joseph, "arose and testified that while President Rigdon was making his first prayer, an angel entered the window and took his seat between Father Smith and himself, and remained there during the prayer."[205] Heber C. Kimball described the angel as "a very tall personage, black eyes, white hair, and stoop shouldered; his garment was whole, extending to near his ankles; on his feet he had sandals. He was sent as a messenger to accept of the dedication."[206] Elder Kimball, in a discourse years later, described the garment worn by this heavenly personage as a "neat woolen garment, nicely adjusted round the neck" and that it was similar to the garment worn by Jesus when he appeared to Joseph Smith in the grove. Fredrick G. Williams also reported that this robe was "without seam,"[207] which was the same description of Moroni's robe when he first appeared to Joseph Smith.[208] We find this description of Jesus's robe in the New Testament (John 19:23). One Latter-day Saint scholar suggested that a seamless robe is "frequently seen as having been typified by the robe of the Mosaic high priest."[209] Elder Kimball also recalled that this angel held "a key in his hand."[210] This heavenly personage was most likely the Apostle Peter. Truman O. Angell explained:

> When about midway during the prayer, there was a glorious sensation passed through the house [Kirtland Temple]; and we, having our heads bowed in prayer, felt a sensation very elevating to the soul. At the close of the prayer, F. [Frederick] G. Williams being in the upper east stand—Joseph being in the speaking stand next below—rose and testified that midway during the prayer an holy angel came and seated himself in the stand. When the afternoon meeting assembled, Joseph, feeling very much elated, arose the first thing and said the personage who had appeared in the morning was the Angel Peter come to accept the dedication.[211]

Eleven-foot-high statue of Apostle Peter holding a key in Capernaum (on the north shore of the Sea of Galilee), photo taken by Trevan Hatch

Joseph Smith recorded that David Whitmer saw several angels present at the dedication of the Kirtland Temple.[212] Elder George A. Smith recalled that Whitmer had seen at least "three angels."[213] Elder Erastus Snow identified these three personages as "Peter, James, and John . . . being seen in the Holy of Holies with golden keys in their hands, in the arch of the temple, and of Joseph saying it was a witness and a testimony that the work of the brethren in building the temple was accepted."[214]

The *Kirtland Council Minute Book* recorded that Joseph Smith was shown by vision the order of how Church councils were conducted in the first century AD. Joseph learned "the law by which to govern the Council in the Church of Christ." He also learned that Jerusalem was the meeting place for the Church council to discuss the affairs of the Church. Joseph saw that the Apostle Peter had been "appointed" by Christ as president of the council and that he held the keys of the kingdom of God on the earth. In addition, Joseph saw that Peter had appointed two counselors to preside in the council if he were ever absent, and that decisions were finalized and callings were issued by a sustaining vote from the members of the council.[215]

Israel Barlow, one of the Prophet's bodyguards, was passing by the temple on his horse three days following the temple dedication (March 30, 1836) when the Prophet Joseph and Oliver Cowdery exited the temple and proceeded down the east walkway. Israel thought he saw Joseph wearing a white suit, but as he approached, he discovered that the Prophet's suit was black. Oliver looked extremely pale and weak as Joseph assisted him towards the gate. Joseph said, "Brother Barlow, Oliver has just been blessed with a great manifestation and he is not as used to this as I am, so it has been almost too much for him." Joseph also commented that, because of what they saw, he would deliver the

Kirtland Temple

"greatest sermon" of his life the next Sunday, April 3, 1836.[216] This day is well known in the Church as the day that Joseph and Oliver were visited by Christ, Elijah, Elias, and Moses.

Joseph also reportedly saw the lives of many prominent martyrs in history. In 1834, after reading the classic, *Fox's Book of Martyrs*, Joseph wrote, "I have, by the aid of the Urim and Thummim [seer stone], seen those martyrs, and they were honest, devoted followers of Christ, according to the light they possessed, and they will be saved."[217] These martyrs include apostles and leaders of the early Church: Stephen, James ("the Great"), Philip, Matthew, James ("the Less"), Matthias, Andrew, Mark, Peter, Paul, Jude, Bartholomew, Thomas, Luke, Simon, John, and Barnabas.[218]

Conclusion

As discussed in this chapter, Joseph Smith was assisted a great deal by ancient prophets. He received a constant flow of manifestations and revelations throughout his life. As many of Joseph's manifestations that are mentioned in this book and others, there are undoubtedly dozens more of which we are unaware. The Prophet Joseph was literally connected with the ancient world and with heaven. Ancient prophets and other angelic personages prepared Joseph for his future work, assisted in the translation of the Book of Mormon, and restored keys and priesthoods. These visitations testify that the Church was restored, not just by a man in his early twenties, but by dozens of divinely appointed prophets who had previously lived on the earth.

Chapter Four

Witnessing the Gold Plates

Joseph Smith testified that he obtained, by assistance of an angel, metallic plates having the appearance of gold, on which was engraved the history of God's dealings with a people in the Western Hemisphere, as well as sacred truths relating to Jesus Christ and salvation. Joseph Smith was not the only person who claimed to have handled or seen the plates. At least twenty-six other individuals saw or handled them as well. This chapter contains several accounts that describe the physical characteristics of the plates, the geographic locations of where they were secured, and the experiences of those who claimed to have seen or handled them. These accounts are an important part of Latter-day Saint history. They add validity to the Prophet Joseph's claims that the plates really existed and provide further details into the shape, size, and weight of the plates.

Joseph Smith's Family and Friends See or Handle the Plates

In late September 1827, a few days after receiving the plates from Moroni, Joseph went to the Hill Cumorah and retrieved the plates from a log where he had hidden them. While walking home, men who apparently knew that Joseph was planning to obtain the plates on this particular night attacked him at least three times.

Joseph warded off the third attacker with a punch that dislocated Joseph's thumb. He then ran the remaining distance (three miles!) to his home while carrying the plates. This incident caused Joseph extreme exhaustion, since the plates weighed approximately sixty pounds.[219] Joseph's mother preserved details of what transpired after Joseph started home with the plates:

> Joseph took the plates from their place and, wrapping them in his linen frock, put them under his arm and started for the house. After walking a short distance in the road, he thought it would be safer to go across through the woods. Traveling some distance after he left the road, he came to a large windfall, and as he was jumping over a log, a man sprang up from behind and gave him a heavy blow with a gun. Joseph turned around and knocked him to the ground, and then ran at the top of his speed. About half a mile further, he was attacked again in precisely the same way. He soon brought this one down also and ran on again, but before he got home, he was accosted the third time with a severe stroke with a gun. When he struck the last one, he dislocated his thumb, which, however, he did not notice till he came in sight of the house. He threw himself down in the corner of the fence to recover his breath. As soon as he was able, he rose and finished his race for the house, where he arrived altogether speechless from fright and fatigue of running.[220]

Lucy Mack Smith

As he entered the house, Joseph's sister Katharine "took the plates from him and laid them on the table, temporarily, and helped revive him until he got breathing properly."[221] As soon as Joseph rested a little, he walked into the kitchen where his father, Joseph Knight, and Josiah Stowell were talking. He showed them his thumb and said, "I must stop talking Father and get you to put my thumb in place for it is very painful."[222] Meanwhile,

Joseph's siblings became restless and eagerly asked if they could remove the plates from the linen cloth. "No," answered Joseph as he put his hands on the plates, "I am instructed not to show them to anyone. If I do, I will transgress and lose them again."[223] Father Smith overhearing the answer said, "What, Joseph, can we not see them?" "No," Joseph replied, "I was disobedient the first time, but I intend to be faithful this time. For I was forbidden to show them until they are translated, but you can feel them."[224] Katharine had also assumed that Joseph would let her see the plates. "We had supposed," she recalled, "that when he should bring them home, the whole family would be allowed to see them, but he said it was forbidden of the Lord. They could be seen only by those who were chosen to bear their testimony to the world. We had therefore to be content until they were translated and we could have the book to read."[225] Soon after he arrived, Joseph permitted his family to handle the plates while they remained in a pillowcase.[226] Among those present were Father and Mother Smith and their children: Hyrum, William, Samuel, Katharine, Sophronia, Don Carlos, and Lucy. Joseph's wife, Emma, and family friends Josiah Stowell and Joseph Knight were also present.

In August 1838, eleven years following that memorable night, Sally Parker, a neighbor, wrote a letter to Francis Tufts recounting a conversation she had with Lucy Smith.

> I lived by [Joseph's] mother, and [she] was one of the finest of women, always helping them that stood in need. She told me the whole story. The plates was [*sic*] in the house and sometimes in the woods for eight months on account of people trying to get them. They had to hide them. Once they hid them under the hearth. They took up the brick and put them in and put the bricks back. The old lady told me this herself with tears in her eyes, and they ran down her cheeks too. She put her hand upon her stomach and said she has the peace of God that rested upon us, all that time. She said it was a heaven below. I asked her if she saw the plates. She said no, it was not for her to see them, but she hefted and handled them, and I believed all she said,

> for I lived by her eight months, and she was one of the best of women.[227]

In 1843, Martha L. Campbell wrote a letter, which was partially dictated by Josiah Stowell, to Joseph Smith Jr. stating, "If I understood him right [Mr. Stoal] was the first person that took the plates out of your hands the morning you brought them in."[228] Josiah Stowell claimed, as did Katharine Smith, that they took the plates from Joseph as he entered the house. Regardless of who took them from Joseph, the fact remains that both of them were permitted to handle the plates.

Emma also handled the plates on many occasions as she helped Joseph translate for a short time. In 1879, Emma answered many questions regarding the translation process and the plates in an interview with her son Joseph Smith III. One of the questions asked was, "Are you sure that he [Joseph Smith Jr.] had the plates at the time you were writing for him?" "The plates," replied Emma, "often lay on the table without any attempt at concealment, wrapped in a small linen tablecloth, which I had given him to fold them in. I once felt of the plates, as they thus lay on the table, tracing their outline and shape. They seemed to be pliable like thick paper, and would rustle with a metallic sound when the edges were moved by the thumb, as one does sometimes thumb the edges of a book."[229]

A few days following Joseph's arrival with the plates, Alva Beaman, a friend and neighbor, assisted Joseph in hiding the plates beneath the hearth at the Smith home. Joseph Noble reported that Beaman was "a man well off as to houses and lands" and that he was "very highly esteemed among men for his word." He also reported that Beaman was permitted to handle the plates while covered as they placed them beneath the hearth.[230] Lucy Mack Smith recalled,

> Joseph came to the house in great haste and inquired if there had been a company of men about. I told him not a single individual had come to the house since he left. He then said that a mob

> would be there that night, if they did not come before that time, to search for the Record, and that it must be removed immediately. Soon afterwards, a man by the name of Beaman came in from the village of Livonia, a man in whom we reposed much confidence, and who was well worthy of the same. Joseph told him his apprehensions of a mob being there that night and that they must prepare themselves to drive them away; but that the first thing to be attended to was to secure the Record and breast-plate. In view of this, it was determined that a portion of the hearth should be taken up and that the Record and breast-plate should be buried under the same, and then the hearth be relaid, to prevent suspicion.[231]

Joseph sought continually to protect the plates as Moroni had commanded him. In the fall of 1827, an angel warned Joseph that a mob was coming to steal away the plates that were hidden in the floor. Joseph then transferred them to his father's shop. Martin Harris remembered that Joseph first hid the plates "in the box under the shop floor: but having been warned by an angel, he removed the plates and hid them in the chamber of the cooper's shop among the flax. That night a mob took up the floor, and dug up the earth, and would have found the plates had they not been removed."[232]

Martin Harris was another individual who saw and handled the plates. He saw them as one of the Three Witnesses, and he handled them while helping Joseph find a hiding place. Harris specifically stated that he held the plates on his knee for an "hour-and-a-half, whilst in conversation with Joseph, when we went to bury them in the woods."[233] Harris's dedication and loyalty to Joseph revealed itself in his hard work and sacrifice in assisting in the translation. Harris's wife, Lucy, however, made it difficult for him to assist Joseph in the translation because of her constant fault-finding. The Lord, attempting to appease her curiosity and doubt, showed her the plates in a dream. Lucy Smith related the experience of Lucy Harris as follows:

> The next morning, soon after she arose, she related a very remarkable dream which she said she had had during the night. . . . She

> said that a personage appeared to her who told her that as she had disputed the servant of the Lord, and said his word was not to be believed, and had also asked him many improper questions, she had done that which was not right in the sight of God. After which he said to her, "Behold, here are the plates, look upon them and believe."
>
> After giving us an account of her dream, she described the Record very minutely, then told us that she had made up her mind in relation to the course which she intended to pursue; namely, that she had in her possession twenty-eight dollars which she received from her mother just before she died, while she was on her death bed, and that Joseph should accept of it.[234]

In the winter months of 1828, Lucy once again became critical of both her husband and Joseph. She was frustrated that they would not allow her to handle and see the plates. One day Lucy demanded her husband to take her to the Smith home in Pennsylvania, which he did. Lucy Smith recorded the following details:

> As soon as she arrived there, she informed him that her object in coming, was to see the plates, and that she would never leave until she had accomplished it. Accordingly, without delay, she commenced ransacking every nook and corner about the house—chests, trunks, cupboards, etc.; consequently, Joseph was under the necessity of removing both the breast-plate and the Record from the house, and secreting them elsewhere. Not finding them in the house, she concluded that Joseph had buried them, and the next day she commenced searching out of doors, which she continued to do until about two o'clock p. m. She then came in rather ill-natured; after warming herself a little, she asked Joseph's wife if there were snakes in that country in the winter. She replied in the negative. Mrs. Harris then said, "I have been walking round in the woods to look at the situation of your place, and as I turned round to come home, a tremendous black snake stuck up his head before me, and commenced hissing at me."
>
> The woman was so perplexed and disappointed in all her undertakings, that she left the house and took lodgings during her stay in Pennsylvania with a near neighbor, to whom she stated that the day previous she had been hunting for the plates, and that, after a tedious search, she at length came to a spot where

> she judged, from the appearance of things, they must be buried; but upon stooping down to scrape away the snow and leaves, in order to ascertain the fact, she encountered a horrible black snake which gave her a terrible fright, and she ran with all possible speed to the house.[235]

Apparently, Joseph eventually permitted Lucy and her daughter to lift the plates while they were inside a box. "My daughter," recalled Martin, "said they [the plates] were about as much as she could lift. They were now in the glass-box, and my wife said they were very heavy. They both lifted them."[236]

Lyman E. Johnson of Pomfret, Vermont, joined the Church in March 1830. Shortly after, he saw a vision of Moroni and the plates following a prayerful request. Little information exists concerning this incident; however, Brigham Young related the experience of Johnson several years following the settlement of the Saints in the Salt Lake Valley. On June 5, 1859, President Young related the following details in the Salt Lake Tabernacle: "One of the Quorum of twelve—a young man full of faith and good works, prayed, and the vision of his mind was opened, and the angel of God came and laid the plates before him, and he saw and handled them, and saw the angel, and conversed with him as he would with one of his friends."[237]

With the plates in his possession and having received a commandment to translate them, Joseph Smith Jr. went to Fayette, New York, with his wife and Oliver Cowdery to stay at the Peter Whitmer Sr. farm. Here, they were able to finish the translation without much distraction from mobs and curious neighbors. As the weeks passed, Mary M. Whitmer, wife of Peter Whitmer Sr., began feeling overwhelmed because of the increased workload caused by the guests. She questioned whether she wanted her home to be the gathering place for every individual involved in the translation process. One day during this stressful time, Moroni visited Mary and showed her the plates. John C. Whitmer, grandson of Mary, recounted the incident as follows:

> One evening, when (after having done her usual day's work in the house) she went to the barn to milk the cows, she met a stranger carrying something on his back that looked like a knapsack. At first she was a little afraid of him, but when he spoke to her in a kind, friendly tone and began to explain to her the nature of the work which was going on in her house, she was filled with inexpressible joy and satisfaction. He then untied his knapsack and showed her a bundle of plates, which in size and appearance corresponded with the description subsequently given by the witnesses to the Book of Mormon. This strange person turned the leaves of the book of plates over, leaf after leaf, and also showed her the engravings upon them; after which he told her to be patient and faithful in bearing her burden a little longer, promising that if she would do so, she should be blessed; and her reward would be sure, if she proved faithful to the end. The personage then suddenly vanished with the plates, and where he went, she could not tell. From that moment my grandmother was enabled to perform her household duties with comparative ease, and she felt no more inclination to murmur because her lot was hard.[238]

Mary's son David, one of the Three Witnesses, described the same incident. "My mother was going to milk the cows, when she was met out near the yard by the same old man (judging by her description of him) who said to her: 'You have been very faithful and diligent in your labors, but you are tried because of the increase of your toil; it is proper therefore that you should receive a witness that your faith may be strengthened.' Thereupon he showed her the plates."[239]

In May 1833, an angel appeared to Harrison G. Burgess and showed him the gold plates. The angel most likely was Moroni as he held the "keys" to the ancient "record" (D&C 27:5). Burgess related,

> In July 1832, when I first heard the fullness of the gospel proclaimed by Elder Simeon Carter, I was convinced that the scriptures were true and that the Book of Mormon was a divine revelation from heaven. I was baptized and spent the following winter in going to school, working for my board and in meeting with the Saints. In the spring of 1833, I started in company with Brother

> John S. Carter to the State of Vermont, where we labored about two months and then returned to New York State.
>
> On the third Sabbath in May while speaking to a congregation I declared that I knew that the Book of Mormon and the work of God were true. The next day while laboring in the field something seemed to whisper to me, 'Do you know the Book of Mormon is true?' My mind became perplexed and darkened, and I was so tormented in spirit that I left my work and retired into the woods. The misery and distress that I there experienced cannot be described. The tempter all the while seemed to say, 'Do you know the Book of Mormon is true?' I remained in this situation about two hours. Finally I resolved to know, by exercising faith similar to that which the brother of Jared possessed, whether I had proclaimed the truth or not, and commenced praying to the God of heaven for a testimony of these things. Suddenly a glorious personage clothed in white stood before me and exhibited to my view the plates from which the Book of Mormon was taken.[240]

Three Witnesses See Moroni and the Plates

Joseph Smith and Oliver Cowdery must have wondered in amazement as they translated the words of Moroni from the plates. It seemed that Moroni was addressing them directly when he wrote, "And now I, Moroni, have . . . told you . . . that ye may show the plates unto those who shall assist to bring forth this work; And unto three shall they be shown by the power of God. . . . And in the mouth of three witnesses shall these things be established" (Ether 5:1–4, see also 2 Nephi 27:12–13). Following the translation of this passage, Joseph and Oliver understood that the Lord would permit three individuals to see the plates. After praying to know who the Three Witnesses should be, the Lord told Joseph through the Urim and Thummim that Oliver Cowdery, Martin Harris, and David Whitmer "shall have a view of the plates" (D&C 17:1). David Whitmer stated that the manifestation occurred "shortly before the completion of the translation when there were but a few pages left" (June 1829).[241]

The Prophet Joseph wrote to his parents, who were in Manchester, New York, telling them to come to Fayette, New York, and to bring Martin Harris with them. Upon their arrival, the Whitmers invited them to stay at their home. They spent the evening and the next morning discussing the translation of the plates, as well as singing and praying. Lucy Smith recalled the events of the morning following their arrival.

> The next morning, after attending to the usual services, namely, reading, singing and praying, Joseph arose from his knees, and approaching Martin Harris with a solemnity that thrills through my veins to this day, when it occurs to my recollection, said, "Martin Harris, you have got to humble yourself before God this day, that you may obtain a forgiveness of your sins. If you do, it is the will of God that you should look upon the plates, in company with Oliver Cowdery and David Whitmer." In a few minutes after this, Joseph, Martin, Oliver and David, repaired to a grove, a short distance from the house, where they commenced calling upon the Lord.[242]

David Whitmer related an experience just prior to joining the other individuals in the grove. "I was plowing in my field," recalled Whitmer, "when I heard a voice saying, 'Blessed is the name of the Lord and those that keep his commandments.' After I had plowed one more round, the Prophet and Oliver Cowdery came along and said, 'Come and be one of the witnesses.' We passed through a clearing and sat on a log."[243] Joseph described the events following their arrival into the woods as follows:

> I commenced prayer to our Heavenly Father, and was followed by each of the others in succession. We did not at the first trial, however, obtain any answer or manifestation of divine favor in our behalf. We again observed the same order of prayer, each calling on and praying fervently to God in rotation, but with the same result as before. Upon this, our second failure, Martin Harris proposed that he should withdraw himself from us, believing, as he expressed himself, that his presence was the cause of our not obtaining what we wished for.
>
> He accordingly withdrew from us, and we knelt down again, and had not been many minutes engaged in prayer, when presently

> we beheld a light above us in the air, of exceeding brightness; and behold, an angel stood before us. In his hands he held the plates which we had been praying for these to have a view of. He turned over the leaves one by one, so that we could see them, and discern the engravings thereon distinctly. . . . When, immediately afterwards, we heard a voice from out of the bright light above us, saying, "These plates have been revealed by the power of God, and they have been translated by the power of God. The translation of them which you have seen is correct, and I command you to bear record of what you now see and hear."[244]

In 1844, Oliver Cowdery testified of this manifestation in a court setting. Cowdery was no longer a member of the Church and had been practicing law in Michigan. One day in court following his opening statement in a murder trial, the attorney of the opposing side began to harass Cowdery saying, "May it please the court and gentlemen of the jury, I see one Oliver Cowdery is going to reply to my argument. I wish he would tell us something about that golden Bible that Joe Smith dug out of the hill; something about the great fraud he perpetrated upon the American people whereby he gained thousands of dollars. Now he seems to know so much about this poor prisoner, I wonder if he has forgotten all about Joe Smith and his connection with him." Judge C. M. Nielson of Salt Lake City was present when Cowdery responded to the attorney. Nielson related,

> Oliver Cowdery arose, calm as a summer morning. I was within three feet of him. There was no hesitation, no fear, no anger in his voice, as he said: "May it please the court, and gentlemen of the jury, my brother attorney on the other side has charged me with connection with Joseph Smith and the golden Bible. The responsibility has been placed upon me, and I cannot escape reply. Before God and man I dare not deny what I have said, and what my testimony contains as written and printed on the front page of the Book of Mormon. May it please your honor and gentlemen of the jury, this I say, I saw the angel and heard his voice—how can I deny it? It happened in the daytime when the sun was shining bright in the firmament; not in the night when I was asleep. That glorious messenger from heaven, dressed

in white, standing above the ground, in a glory I have never seen anything to compare with, the sun insignificant in comparison, and this personage told us if we denied that testimony there is no forgiveness in this life nor in the world to come. Now how can I deny it—I dare not; I will not!"[245]

David Whitmer also related his experience several years following his excommunication from the Church. Whitmer believed that Joseph was a fallen prophet and had "drifted into error and spiritual blindness."[246] On September 7, 1878, while being interviewed by then Elders Orson Pratt and Joseph F. Smith, Whitmer spoke about the experience of seeing the plates and Moroni.

> *David Whitmer*: Joseph, Oliver and myself were together when I saw them. We not only saw the plates of the Book of Mormon, but also the brass plates, [a Jewish record carried by Lehi's colony from Jerusalem and frequently referred to in the Book of Mormon] the plates of the Book of Ether, the plates containing the record of the wickedness and secret combinations of the people of the world down to the time of their being engraved, and many other plates. The fact is, it was just as though Joseph, Oliver and I were sitting just here on a log, when we were overshadowed by a light. It was not like the light of the sun nor like that of a fire, but more glorious and beautiful. It extended away round us, I cannot tell how far, but in the midst of this light about as far off as he sits (pointing to John C. Whitmer, sitting a few feet from him), there appeared, as it were, a table with many records or plates upon it, besides the plates of the Book of Mormon, also the sword of Laban, the directors, i.e., the ball which Lehi had], and the interpreters. I saw them just as plain as I see this bed (striking the bed beside him with his hand), and I heard the voice of the Lord, as distinctly as I ever heard anything in my life, declaring that the records of the plates of the Book of Mormon were translated by the gift and power of God.
>
> *Orson Pratt*: Did you see the angel this time?
>
> *David Whitmer*: Yes, he stood before us. Our testimony as recorded in the Book of Mormon is strictly and absolutely true, just as it is there written.[247]

Whitmer reported in another interview that they heard the Lord's voice while viewing the plates: "The Lord told us in reply that he would make it known to the people that the early inhabitants of this land had been just such a people as they were described in the [plates] and he would lead them to uncover the ruins of the great cities, and they should have abundant evidence of the truth of that which is written in the book."[248]

After the vision closed, Joseph left Oliver Cowdery and David Whitmer to search for Martin Harris. He soon found him praying away from the initial gathering place. They joined together in prayer and the same vision opened to them. Martin Harris then rejoiced aloud saying, "Tis enough; tis enough; mine eyes have beheld; mine eyes have beheld."[249]

Just prior to his death in July 1875, Harris related to a group of Saints assembled in Clarkson, Utah, his experience in seeing the plates. Harris stated that the angel stood before them and said, "Look" as he showed them the plates. "When I gazed upon him," recalled Harris, "I fell to the earth, but I stood on my feet again and saw the angel turn the golden leaves over, and I said, 'That is enough. My Lord, and my God.' Then I heard the voice of God say: 'The Book translated from those plates is true and translated correctly.'"[250] George Godfrey, a friend of Harris's, sat at his bedside many nights to assist him in his last moments. Godfrey recorded his conversation with Harris a few hours prior to his death:

> When he was so weak and enfeebled that he was unable to recognize me or anyone, and knew not to whom he was speaking, I asked him if he did not feel that there was an element at least, of fraudulence and deception in the things that were written and told of the coming forth of the Book of Mormon, and he replied as he had always done so many, many times in my hearing and with the same spirit he always manifested when enjoying health and vigor and said: "The Book of Mormon is no fake. I know what I know. I have seen what I have seen and I have heard what I have heard. I have seen the gold plates from which the Book of Mormon is written. An angel appeared to me and others and testified to the truthfulness of the record, and had I been willing to have perjured myself and sworn falsely to the testimony I now

> bear I could have been a rich man, but I could not have testified other than I have done and am now doing for these things are true."[251]

Lucy Smith recalled that Joseph and the Three Witnesses arrived home from the grove around four o'clock p.m. Joseph went into the bedroom where his father, mother, and Mrs. Whitmer were sitting. He flung himself on the bed beside his mother and, with an expression of relief, said,

> Father, mother, you do not know how happy I am: the Lord has now caused the plates to be shown to three more besides myself. They have seen an angel, who has testified to them, and they will have to bear witness to the truth of what I have said, for now they know for themselves, that I do not go about to deceive the people, and I feel as if I was relieved of a burden which was almost too heavy for me to bear, and it rejoices my soul, that I am not any longer to be entirely alone in the world.[252]

Eight Witnesses Handle the Plates

The Lord instructed Joseph to show the plates to an additional eight individuals. The day following the manifestation of the plates to Cowdery, Whitmer, and Harris, the Smiths returned home to Manchester; the Whitmers and Oliver Cowdery joined them a few days later. They came to discuss arrangements for the publication of the Book of Mormon and to see the plates, which Joseph had promised some of them. On June 25, 1829, Joseph accompanied eight men into a wooded area where they "looked upon the plates and handled them."[253] These eight individuals were Christian Whitmer, Jacob Whitmer, Peter Whitmer Jr., John Whitmer, Hiram Page, Joseph Smith Sr., Hyrum Smith, and Samuel H. Smith. All of them testified of their experience in written form that they all signed and later published near the introduction page in the Book of Mormon.

> Be it known unto all nations, kindreds, tongues, and people, unto whom this work shall come: that Joseph Smith, Jun., the translator of this work, has shown unto us the plates of which

> hath been spoken, which have the appearance of gold; and as many of the leaves as the said Smith has translated we did handle with our hands; and we also saw the engravings thereon, all of which has the appearance of ancient work, and of curious workmanship. And this we bear record with words of soberness, that the said Smith has shown unto us, for we have seen and hefted, and know of a surety that the said Smith has got the plates of which we have spoken. And we give our names unto the world to witness unto the world that which we have seen. And we lie not, God bearing witness of it.[254]

John Whitmer possibly handled the plates before June 1829 as he had helped in the translation for a short time.[255] In March 1836, Whitmer testified that he saw and handled the plates: "I desire to testify to all that will come to the knowledge of this address; that I have most assuredly seen the plates from whence the Book of Mormon is translated, and that I have handled these plates, and know of a surety that Joseph Smith, Jr. has translated the Book of Mormon by the gift and power of God.[256]

In 1888, Hiram Page's son Philander spoke of his father's testimony of seeing and handling the plates. He also vouched for at least three other individuals who were in the grove when the Prophet Joseph presented the plates.

> I knew my father to be true and faithful to his testimony of the divinity of the Book of Mormon until the very last. Whenever he had an opportunity to bear his testimony to this effect, he would always do so, and seemed to rejoice exceedingly in having been privileged to see the plates and thus become one of the Eight Witnesses. I can also testify that Jacob, John and David Whitmer, and Oliver Cowdery died in full faith in the divinity of the Book of Mormon. I was with all these witnesses on their deathbeds and heard each of them bear his last testimony.[257]

Samuel Smith also claimed to have seen the plates outside of his signed testimony with the other witnesses. On January 25, 1832, the Lord instructed Samuel Smith and Orson Hyde to "take their journey into the eastern countries, and proclaim the things which I have commanded them" (D&C 75:13). A few months later, they traveled to Erie County, Pennsylvania, to preach about the Book of Mormon and relate the experiences of Joseph Smith. Present at one of these meetings was Daniel Tyler. "In the spring of 1832," wrote Tyler, "Elders Samuel H. Smith and Orson Hyde . . . came to our neighborhood and held a few meetings. Elder Smith . . . delineated the circumstances of the coming forth of the Book of Mormon, of which he said he was a witness. He knew his brother Joseph had the plates, for the prophet had shown them to him, and he had handled them and seen the engravings thereon."[258]

In 1839, Hyrum Smith published, in the *Times and Seasons*, his testimony of the Restoration and experience as a Book of Mormon witness. "I had been abused and thrust into a dungeon," wrote Hyrum, "and confined for months on account of my faith, and the testimony of Jesus Christ. However I thank God that I felt a determination to die, rather than deny the things which my eyes had seen, which my hands had handled, and which I had borne testimony to."[259]

A Cave at Cumorah

Moroni did not permit Joseph to keep the plates in his possession following the completion of the translation. Several accounts provide details concerning Joseph returning the plates to Moroni that were stored in a cave at Cumorah. Consider the statement of Brigham Young, delivered in Farmington, Utah, on June 17, 1877.

> I believe I will take the liberty to tell you of another circumstance that will be as marvelous as anything can be. . . . Oliver Cowdery went with the Prophet Joseph when he deposited these plates. Joseph did not translate all of the plates; there was a portion of them sealed, which you can learn from the Book of Doctrine and Covenants. When Joseph got the plates, the angel instructed him to carry them back to the hill Cumorah, which he did. Oliver says that when Joseph and Oliver went there, the hill opened, and they walked into a cave, in which there was a large and spacious

> room. He says he did not think, at the time, whether they had the light of the sun or artificial light; but that it was just as light as day. They laid the plates on a table; it was a large table that stood in the room. Under this table there was a pile of plates as much as two feet high, and there were altogether in this room more plates than probably many wagon loads; they were piled up in the corners and along the walls. The first time they went there the sword of Laban hung upon the wall; but when they went again it had been taken down and laid upon the table across the gold plates; it was unsheathed, and on it was written these words: "This sword will never be sheathed again until the kingdoms of this world become the kingdom of our God and his Christ."[260]

On November 11, 1869, President Young related a similar account to the brethren in the Salt Lake School of the Prophets. Wilford Woodruff was present at the meeting and recorded Brigham's comments.

> President Young said in relation to Joseph Smith returning the plates of the Book of Mormon that he did not return them to the box [at Cumorah] . . . but he went in a cave in the hill Cumorah with Oliver Cowdery and deposited those plates upon a table or shelf. In that room were deposited a large amount of gold plates containing sacred records and when they first visited that room the sword of Laban was hanging upon the wall and when they last visited it, the sword was drawn from the scabbard and [placed] upon a table and a messenger who was the keeper of the room informed them that that sword would never be returned to its scabbard until the Kingdom of God was Established upon the earth and until it reigned triumphant over every enemy. Joseph Smith said that cave contained tons of choice treasures and records.[261]

Perhaps the earliest known account regarding the cave at Cumorah is in the diary of William H. Dame, dated January 14, 1855. Dame heard President Young relate the details as told to him by Hyrum Smith. "Joseph, Hyrum, Cowdery, Whitmer," recorded Dame, "went to the hill Cumorah. As they were walking up the hill, a door opened and they walked into a room about 16 ft. square. In that room was an angel and a trunk. On the trunk lay a Book of Mormon & Gold Plates, Laban's sword, Aaron's Breastplate."[262]

Brigham Young said that "Whitmer" was one of the men who went into the cave; however, David Whitmer told Edward Stevenson in 1877 that he did not visit the cave. Stevenson was told that "Oliver Cowdery told him that the Prophet Joseph and himself had seen this room and that it was filled with treasure, and on a table therein were the breast plate and the sword of Laban, as well as the portion of the gold plates not yet translated, and that these plates were bound by three small gold rings."[263] Either President Young had forgotten the details of the event or one of David's brothers accompanied the Prophet to the cave. In an interview published in 1878, P. Wilhelm Poulson asked David Whitmer, "Where are the plates now?" "In a cave," replied David, "where the angel has hidden them up till the time arrives when the plates, which are sealed, shall be translated."[264]

Heber C. Kimball also spoke about the cave. While relating details regarding the Saints crossing the plains in a meeting on September 28, 1856, Elder Kimball stated, "How does it compare with the vision that Joseph and others had, when they went into a cave in the hill Cumorah, and saw more records than ten men could carry? There were books piled up on tables, book upon book. Those records this people will yet have, if they accept of the Book of Mormon and observe its precepts, and keep the commandments."[265] Years later while speaking to a group in the Church Historian's office, Elder Kimball stated that Father Smith also accompanied Joseph to the cave. "Father Smith, Oliver Cowdery, and others," recalled Elder Kimball, "[walked] into the Hill Cumorah and [saw] records upon records piled upon the tables, they walked from cell to cell and saw the records that were piled up."[266]

The following experience of Joseph Smith, Oliver Cowdery, and David Whitmer provide additional information in light of the aforementioned accounts. In June 1829—before the Three Witnesses saw Moroni and the plates in the official setting—Joseph, Cowdery, and Whitmer were returning from Harmony, Pennsylvania, to Fayette, New York, when they encountered Moroni en route to Cumorah. Whitmer offered the details.

> When I was returning to Fayette, with Joseph and Oliver, all of us riding in the wagon, . . . a very pleasant, nice looking old man suddenly appeared by the side of our wagon and saluted us with, "Good morning; it is very warm;" at the same time wiping his face or forehead with his hand. We returned the salutation, and by a sign from Joseph, I invited him to ride if he was going our way. But he said very pleasantly, "No, I am going to Cumorah." This name was somewhat new to me, and I did not know what "Cumorah" meant. We all gazed at him and at each other, and as I looked round inquiringly of Joseph, the old man instantly disappeared, so that I did not see him again.[267]

Whitmer recalled, in another account, that the "nice looking man" was about "5 feet 10, heavy set and on his back an old fashioned army knapsack strapped over his shoulders and something square in it." Whitmer also remembered turning around to inquire of Joseph concerning this "Cumorah" and seeing his complexion "as white as a sheet." The Prophet told Cowdery and Whitmer that the man "was one of the Nephites, and that he had the plates."[268] In a third account, Whitmer explained that Moroni was "dressed in a suit of brown woolen clothes, his hair and beard were white. . . . that he had on his back sort of a knapsack with something, shaped like a book. It was the messenger who had the plates, who had taken them from Joseph just prior to our starting from Harmony."[269]

Although these accounts of a cave at Cumorah appear in early LDS sources, we must read them with caution. First, all of the accounts about the cave were written more than twenty-five years after these few individuals were thought to have seen the cave, and most accounts are dated to the 1870s, nearly fifty years later. Second, all existing accounts are attributed to individuals who were not present at the cave and were not yet associated with Joseph Smith. That neither Joseph Smith nor his mother mentioned the cave at Cumorah is also telling, considering the numerous other details they provided about the plates and events during this time. Perhaps a few options regarding these accounts are (1) they describe an actual cave at Cumorah; (2) they describe a vision that some saw of where the plates were located, and assumed it was Cumorah (or later commentators assumed the location was Cumorah); (3) a myth or supposition was perpetuated by someone in the 1850s that the plates were stored in a cave at Cumorah and, to increase credibility, attributed the details to Joseph Smith (note that numerous early Latter-day Saints attributed fanciful and sensational sayings to Joseph Smith that cannot be corroborated by other, more reliable sources).

Descriptions of the Gold Plates

Joseph Smith recorded that the plates had the "appearance of gold," and that they were "six inches wide and eight inches long and not quite so thick as common tin. They were . . . bound together in a volume, as the leaves of a book with three rings running through the whole. The volume was something near six inches in thickness, a part of which was sealed."[270] After lifting the plates, wrapped in cloth, William Smith estimated its weight at approximately "sixty pounds." He also recalled the following details: "They were fastened together by rings running through the back"[271] and "were not quite as large as this Bible. . . . [We] could raise the leaves this way (raising a few leaves of the Bible before him). One could easily tell that they were not stone, hewn out to deceive, or even a block of wood. Being a *mixture of gold and copper*, they were much heavier than stone, and very much heavier than wood."[272]

David Whitmer recorded a similar description of the plates: they had the appearance of "gold," they were "about six by nine inches in size—about as thick as parchment," and they were "bound together like the leaves of a book by massive rings passing through the back edges."[273] John Whitmer described the plates as containing "three rings, each one in the shape of a D with the straight line towards the center."[274] After Moroni showed Mary Whitmer the plates, she similarly described them to her son David as being "fastened with rings, thus" (following Mary's description came a drawing of a "D").[275] Orson Pratt also commented on the rings that bound the metallic leaves: "Through the back of the plates were three rings, which held them together, and through which a rod might easily be passed, serving as a greater convenience for carrying them."[276]

Joseph Smith explained that the engravings on plates were "Egyptian characters . . . [that] were small, and beautifully engraved. The whole book exhibited many marks of antiquity in its construction and much skill in the art of engraving."[277] The writing was similar to Hebrew in that it read from right to left.[278] Orson Pratt also recorded that the plates had "fine engravings, which were stained with a black, hard stain, so as to make the letters more legible and easier to be read."[279] On February 17, 1834, Charles Anthon, to whom Martin Harris showed a portion of the engravings traced on a piece of paper, described them in a letter to E. D. Howe.

> This paper . . . consisted of all kinds of singular characters disposed in columns, and had evidently been prepared by some person who had before him at the time a book containing various alphabets, Greek and Hebrew letters, crosses and flourishes; Roman letters inverted or placed sideways were arranged and placed in perpendicular columns, and the whole ended in a rude delineation of a circle, divided into various compartments, arched with various strange marks, and evidently copied after the Mexican calendar.[280]

Seven years after later, Anthon wrote a letter to a Rev. Coit in which he described the characters on the plates: "The characters were arranged in columns like the Chinese mode of writing, and presented the most singular medley that I ever beheld. Greek, Hebrew, and all sorts of letters, more or less distorted, either through unskilfullness or from actual designs, were intermingled with sundry delineations of half moons, stars, and other natural objects, and the whole ended in a rude representation of the Mexican Zodiac."[281]

Recent Discoveries of Metallic Plates

Critics of Joseph Smith have doubted that ancient writings were engraved on metallic plates and have assumed large national records were only preserved on papyri, parchment, or stone. Note, however, that several metallic documents have been discovered; specifically, at least three separate gold-plated records were discovered within the last seventy years and have become known only recently. These documents provide us with more details concerning ancient writing practices. The record of Lehi's posterity was engraved on metallic plates made by Nephi in the sixth century BC and Mormon in the fourth century AD. An article in the *Journal of Book of Mormon Studies* reported that a gold book was discovered in October 2005 in Tehran, Iran. The plates contain "eight gold sheets inscribed in cuneiform script, which was used in much of the ancient Near East." These plates were "bound by four small rings passing through holes in the sheets" and dates to the sixth century BC, around the time Lehi's family left Jerusalem.[282] A similar ancient gold metallic book with Etruscan[283] writing was discovered in southwestern Bulgaria (located near Greece and Turkey) in the 1940s. The soldier who discovered this book donated it to the National Museum of History in Sofia, Bulgaria, in 2003. This record also dates to around the sixth century BC and is possibly the "oldest complete book in the world."[284]

A third set of metallic records dating to the second century AD was discovered in 1986 in Dacia (present-day Romania). Latter-day Saint antiquities dealers and donors acquired the ancient plates and displayed them at Brigham Young University's Harold B. Lee Library in 2007. These ancient Roman plates are similar in description to the fourth-century AD plates that Joseph

Smith obtained. The record consists of two metallic plates that are approximately "five inches by seven inches" in size with each plate being approximately "one sixteenth of an inch thick." This is similar to the description of the Nephite plates as being "six inches wide and eight inches long and not quite so thick as common tin" (see descriptions above). The two Roman plates were connected, similar to the Book of Mormon plates, by metal rings passing through the edge of the plates and were made of "an alloy of copper and tin." In a similar manner, the plates, according to William Smith, were "a mixture of gold and copper." The Roman plates also contain the names of "seven witnesses" who signed the legal document in order to "authenticate the record." As previously mentioned, the ancient prophet Nephi spoke of "three" men who would become "witnesses" to his record (2 Nephi 27:12). John W. Welch and Kelsey D. Lambert at Brigham Young University posited that the practice of witnesses signing their names to authenticate a document is "consonant with biblical and Jewish Law (Deuteronomy 19:15)." Perhaps the most fascinating similarity between the fourth-century Nephite plates and the second-century Roman plates is that they both contained a sealed portion that could not be read unless the seal was broken.[285]

Conclusion

Critics of Joseph Smith and Mormonism have always attempted to repudiate the testimonies of the Three and Eight Witnesses to the Book of Mormon. Dan Vogel, a critic of Joseph Smith, has developed new arguments to discredit claims of Joseph and the witnesses. For instance, Vogel suggested that Joseph made "the plates out of tin" and etched in ancient looking characters to deceive people.[286] He also argued that the witnesses simply saw "hallucinations."[287] Should we believe, however, that the Three and Eight Witnesses saw the same hallucination at the same time? Vogel would say yes. He posited that Joseph, being a hypnotist and a magician, caused his earliest followers to enter into hypnotic trances simultaneously[288] and that he deceived them with "trickery."[289] As another possibility, Vogel suggested that all of the witnesses might have hallucinated together due to low blood sugar from "fasting."[290]

Critics like Vogel have discovered that proving false the testimonies of the Book of Mormon witnesses is difficult because, among other reasons, all of the witnesses were well-respected men in their communities who never recanted their claims. Some non-LDS scholars, therefore, have abandoned the argument that the witnesses conspired with Joseph, or were deceived by Joseph, to perpetuate a massive fraud. This does not fit with what we know about Joseph Smith. Several prominent historians take Joseph at his word and accept that he experienced at least "something." For example, Richard Mouw, an Evangelical scholar, conveyed his struggle with the story of Joseph Smith.

> My instinct is to attribute a sincerity to Joseph Smith, and yet at the same time, as an Evangelical Christian, I do not believe that the members of the Godhead really appeared to him and told him that he should start on a mission . . . of denouncing the kinds of things that I believe as a Presbyterian. I can't believe that. And yet, at the same time, I really don't believe that he was simply making up a story that he knew to be false in order to manipulate people and to gain power over a religious movement. And so, I live with the mystery.[291]

Mouw, having studied Joseph Smith, understands that one cannot so easily explain away Joseph's claims. He is willing to leave open the possibility that Joseph was sincere and that he really experienced supernatural manifestations.

Robert Remini, emeritus professor of History at the University of Illinois at Chicago, is another non-LDS historian who understands the complexity of Joseph Smith's story and is willing to engage in the particulars of his history.

> I must admit that even before I began a serious study of Joseph Smith's life, I rather liked the man. I thought him a courageous and brave individual who achieved something quite remarkable.

> Moreover, he sacrificed his life for what he believed. As I studied him for several years, I came to admire him the more I got to know him . . . I frankly do not support the transnational concept in trying to explain Joseph Smith and who he was. Quite obviously, by founding a religion that has survived for almost two centuries, the Prophet did, in fact, place Mormonism in the great stream of the history of Christianity. . . . Mormonism has expanded, has been accepted, and has become part of the Christian tradition.[292]

Latter-day Saints do not expect everyone to accept blindly the claims of Joseph Smith and the witnesses. We do hope, however, that non-Latter-day Saints will understand that our history is complex and contains thousands of personal journals, many of which were recorded shortly after the events occurred. A combination of these personal memoirs creates a realistic picture of what Joseph Smith and the witnesses experienced. Their histories do not remove all doubt, but they smack of enough reality that some scholars are willing to engage them rather than dismiss and ignore them.

Chapter Five

Seer Stones, a Urim and Thummim, and the Restoration

Seer stones and a Urim and Thummim played a major role in the Restoration. Joseph Smith received a Urim and Thummim the same day he obtained the plates, and Moroni commanded him to use it to translate the ancient record. Joseph also possessed seer stones that the Lord sanctioned for revelatory and translating purposes. This chapter provides explanations of ancient seer stones and the biblical Urim and Thummim, how the seer stones and the Urim and Thummim were used in early Church history, and the revelations and visions Joseph received through these instruments.

Ancient Seer Stones and the Biblical Urim and Thummim

We know from seven passages in the Old Testament that the Israelites used a certain object in the temple called the Urim and Thummim.[293] The high priest kept this instrument in his possession and used it to understand the will of God and to foresee future events (see Exodus 28; Numbers 27:21).[294] The Lord instructed the high priest to wear, as sacred holy vestments, "a breastplate, and an ephod, and a robe, and a broidered coat, a

The Israelite high priest dressed in the temple vestments,
courtesy of Dan McClellan

mitre, and a girdle" (Exodus 28:4). The ephod, made of gold, blue, purple, and scarlet material, was draped over the shoulders with the sides joined together. The breastplate containing twelve pouches, each holding a precious stone bearing a name of a tribe, was placed over the ephod. The Lord instructed the high priest to fasten the Urim and Thummim to the breastplate and construct a pouch in which the Urim and Thummim could be placed. The pouch was most likely located behind the twelve stones in the middle of the breastplate, as the Lord instructed the high priest to place it over the "heart" (see Exodus 28:30).

If any man desired to receive instruction from the Lord, he would approach the high priest and request him to inquire of the Lord through the Urim and Thummim. If the high priest inquired for any individual who was unclean in spirit, the Urim and Thummim would remain dark (see Numbers 27:21; 1 Samuel 28:6). The Jerusalem Talmud—an ancient body of authoritative Jewish discussions and writings regarding Jewish custom, law, and history—explains that this ancient Israelite revelatory instrument is "called *Urim*, derived from *or*, 'light,' because they light the way for Israel, showing them what course to follow; *Tumim*, cognate to *tamim*, 'whole,' because they make the way 'whole' before them. For when the children of Israel were 'whole,' that is, righteous, the *Urim* and *Tumim* would direct them along the proper path."[295] Not only must the individual approaching the high priest be clean, but the high priest himself must be clean and possess the Holy Spirit when approaching the Lord through the Urim and Thummim. The Babylonian Talmud, a text similar to the one just cited, posits that, "To any priest who does not speak through the Holy Spirit and upon whom the Divine Presence does not rest, they do not bring the inquiry."[296]

According to an ancient Jewish legend, "If the high priest was worthy, he received an answer to every inquiry, for on these stones were engraved all the letters of the alphabet, so that all conceivable words could be constructed from them."[297] After the high priest inquired through the Urim and Thummim, the answer would appear in the twelve stones located in the breastplate.[298] Each stone contained an engraved name of one of the twelve tribes of Israel. According to legend, several letters in these names would become illumined, thus forming a word and the answer to the inquiry.[299] For example, in the names Zebulon, Naphtali, and Levi, the letters "b," "t," and "L" were illumined and the priest would render the name as "Bethel" (note that there were no vowels in Hebrew). According to Jewish tradition, the Urim and Thummim ceased working following the destruction of the first Temple in the sixth century BC.[300]

The Urim and Thummim in ancient Israel was similar to the Urim and Thummim that the prophet Mosiah possessed, which was passed down to him and eventually delivered to Joseph Smith. The Book of Mormon explains that the Urim and Thummim, "were *prepared from the beginning*, and were handed down from generation to generation, for the purpose of *interpreting languages*; and they have been kept and preserved by the hand of the Lord" (Mosiah 28:14–15; emphasis added). Mosiah 8:13 also refers to the Urim and Thummim, "called interpreters," that are used to "translate all records that are of ancient date; and it is a gift from God." The brother of Jared originally possessed this Urim and Thummim and brought it to the Americas. Each generation inherited the interpreters until it finally ended up in Moroni's possession. In what is now upstate New York, Moroni eventually buried the Urim and Thummim with the breastplate and the gold plates in the fifth century AD. After the Lord gave the "two stones" to the brother of Jared, he received the following instruction:

> Behold, thou shalt not suffer these things which ye have seen and heard to go forth unto the world. . . .
>
> And behold, when ye shall come unto me, ye shall write them and shall seal them up, that no one can interpret them; for ye shall write them in a language that they cannot be read.
>
> And behold, these two stones will I give unto thee, and ye shall seal them up also with the things which ye shall write.
>
> For behold, the language which ye shall write I have

> confounded; wherefore I will cause in my own due time that these stones shall magnify to the eyes of men these things which ye shall write. (Ether 3:21–24)

We also read in Ether concerning sixteen stones of the same qualities as the Urim and Thummim. These stones were "white and clear" like that of "transparent glass." The brother of Jared laid the stones before God and he touched them and they did "shine forth in darkness" (Ether 3:1–4). Notice the similarities between these stones and the seer stone mentioned in Alma 37:23, which did "shine forth in darkness." These sixteen stones provided light to small barges that transported the Jaredites across the ocean.[301] Note that Noah, in Jewish tradition, possessed a stone that provided light in the ark similar to the Jaredite barges. Genesis 6:16 mentions a "window" in the ark. The Hebrew word for "window" (*tsohar*) in this passage literally translates as "gleam," "shine," or "illuminate." *Tsohar* can also be translated as "noon" or even "bright of happiness."[302] Some rabbis believed that the "window" was actually a "precious stone, the light of which was more brilliant by night than by day, so enabling Noah to distinguish between day and night" while in the ark.[303] Also note that the word *light* comes from the Hebrew word *Urim*. Orson Pratt posited that the Lord provided Noah a Urim and Thummim to show him how to build the ark. "Noah," stated Pratt, "after having preached the Gospel and published glad tidings among the nations, was commanded to build an ark. He had a Urim and Thummim by which he was enabled to discern all things pertaining to the ark and its pattern."[304]

Scattered traditions also suggest that Adam, Abraham, and other ancient patriarchs possessed stones that were used for the purpose of conversing with angels and receiving dreams and visions.[305] The Book of Abraham reveals that Abraham did possess a Urim and Thummim (see Abraham 3:2–5) and that he saw visions in it of the stars.

The ancient Americas also produced traditions of spiritual

stones. Israel Worsley gathered information from Spanish records and chronicles regarding fifteenth- and sixteenth-century Native American tribes. In 1828, he published a book that contained much of his research. In this book he discussed legends of a "transparent stone" similar to the Urim and Thummim. This stone "possessed great power to bring down rain, when put into a basin of water, agreeable to a divine virtue impressed on one of them in times of old." He also explained that this stone would "suffer injury if it were seen by any common person;" and if this stone were seen by any "foreigner," meaning an enemy from another land, the stone "would lose all its divine power." He further reported that some of these Native American tribes built temples. Each of these temples contained "a holy place in to which none may enter but the priest, and he only on particular occasions—there he makes a yearly atonement for sin, dressed in a fantastic garb, which is a humble imitation of the High Priest's robes, with a *breast plate and other ornaments*." These Native Americans also perpetuated legends of a "holy book," which they had lost and therefore, "fell under the displeasure of the Great Spirit." Worsley transmitted their belief that one day they will regain their "holy book" and "transparent stone" and are "looking for and expecting someone to come and teach them the right way."[306]

Joseph Smith's Urim and Thummim

On September 22, 1827, Joseph Smith received the plates, a Urim and Thummim, and a breastplate. Like the prophets of old, Joseph used the Urim and Thummim to understand the will of the Lord on certain matters, as well as to translate ancient documents. Joseph described the Urim and Thummim as consisting "of two transparent stones set in the rim of a bow."[307] Upon examining the Urim and Thummim, Lucy Smith recorded that the stones were "smooth three-cornered diamonds set in glass, and the glasses were set in silver bows, which were connected with each other in much the same way as old-fashioned spectacles."[308]

Martin Harris described the spectacles as being "two inches in diameter, perfectly round, and about five-eighths of an inch thick at the center; but not so thick at the edges where they came into the bow. They were joined by a round bar of silver, about three-eighths of an inch in diameter, and about four inches long, which, with the two stones, would make eight inches." He then described the stones as "white, like polished marble, with a few gray streaks." Harris feared that if he looked into them he would "perish."[309] A passage in the Book of Mormon states that "no man can look in them [interpreters] except he be commanded, lest he should look for that he ought not and he should perish. And whosoever is commanded to look in them, the same is called seer" (Mosiah 8:13). William Smith recalled that the Urim and Thummim was attached to the breastplate and, similar to the Urim and Thummim mentioned in Exodus 28, "A pocket was prepared in the breastplate on the left side, immediately over the heart" in which the Urim and Thummim was placed. William also reported that the Urim and Thummim could be "detached from the breastplate . . . but [Joseph] always used it in connection with the breastplate when receiving official communications, and usually so when translating, as it permitted him to have both hands free."[310]

Joseph Smith's Gift as a Seer

A few days after receiving the plates and the Urim and Thummim, the Prophet Joseph described them to Joseph Knight. "After breakfast," recalled Knight, "Joseph called me into the other room. . . . He set his foot on the bed, leaned his head on his hand and said . . . 'It is ten times better than I expected.' Then he went on to tell length and width and thickness of the plates; and said he, 'They appear to be gold.' But he seemed to think more of the glasses or the Urim and Thummim than he did of the plates, for, said he, 'I can see anything; they are marvelous.'"[311] Joseph also acquired at least three seer stones

Joseph Smith Jr.

before receiving the plates from Moroni. Joseph found a dark-colored stone while digging a well for Willard Chase in 1822.[312] E. W. Vanderhoof described Joseph's other stone as being "whitish, glossy, and opaque."[313] The third stone that Joseph supposedly received from Jack Belcher was "a green stone, with brown, irregular spots on it."[314]

Joseph discovered at an early age that he could often see images in the stones. As a result, he began associating with individuals who claimed that treasures were buried in the earth in various places throughout the region. The generation of the late eighteenth through the early nineteenth century experienced a heightened interest in the practice of treasure digging and folk magic. Benjamin Franklin described the popularity and procedures of treasure digging that were so pervasive at this time: "You can hardly walk half a Mile out of Town on any Side without observing several Pits dug with that Design, and perhaps some lately opened. Men, otherwise of very good Sense, have been drawn into this Practice. . . . There seems to be some peculiar Charm in the conceit of finding money."[315] Ronald Walker, a Latter-day Saint historian, explained the phenomenon of "treasure digging" as follows:

> From colonial time to at least the Age of Jackson, Americans dug for magical treasure. There were hundreds and probably thousands of these "money diggers," all seeking troves of fabled coins, mines, jewels, and other valued prizes. They worked from the Atlantic Coast to the Mississippi hinterlands and in a few localities heaped up tailings that rivaled those of the later forty-niners. Yet, for all this prodigious toil, their "finds" were as rare as Merlin's transmuted gold. What made them persist? Relying on an immemorial but now forgotten world view, the money diggers placed faith in conjuring, elemental spirits, thrice-spoken dreams, seeric gifts, and enchanted treasure that could slip and rumble through the earth as easily as a fish moving through the deep. The modern age will probably never fully understand the diggers' strange compound of treasure seeking, religious feeling, and intense psychological devotion to an old but fading way of life. Theirs was another world which we can speak of but hardly enter.[316]

An article in the *Palmyra Reflector* in 1831 also recognized the ubiquity of treasure digging with the use of occult objects.

> Men and women, without distinction of age or sex, became marvelous wise in the occult sciences, many dreamed, and others saw visions disclosing to them deep in the bowels of the earth, rich and shining treasures, and to facilitate those mighty mining operations, (money was usually if not always sought after in the night time,) divers devices and implements were invented. . . . Mineral rods and balls, (as they were called by the impostor who made use of them,) were supposed to be infallible guides to these sources of wealth—"PEEP STONES" or pebbles, taken promiscuously from the brook or field, were placed in a hat or other situation excluded from the light, when some [individual] applied their eyes . . . , declared they saw all the wonders of nature, including of course, ample stores of silver and gold.[317]

Walker explained that individuals who participated in these magic activities, considered them as practices of the "white art" and not of the black art: "Most Old World magical practitioners warmly rejected any league with the powers of darkness. Their craft was beneficium, the white art, which opposite devilish compacts, consorting with demons, and the works of evil witches."[318] Richard Bushman suggested that many individuals, "yearning for contact with powers beyond this world" and hoping "for a return of primitive Christianity's divine gifts," turned to "stone gazing, treasure hunting, and spiritualism."[319] Members of the Smith family were among those who engaged in white art activities including Joseph Smith Jr., who, unknowingly at the time, possessed the gift of a seer. Regarding Joseph's gift, Josiah Stowell testified in court that Joseph had the ability to see "fifty feet" below ground. Upon hearing the testimony, Justice Neeley said, "Deacon Stowell, do I understand you as swearing before God, under the solemn oath you have taken, that you believe the prisoner can see by the aid of the stone fifty feet below the surface of the earth, as plainly as you can see what is on my table?" Stowell replied, "Do I believe it? No, it is not a matter of belief. I positively know it to be true."[320]

A book on American religious culture, published by the University of North Carolina Press, recognized that "[Joseph Smith] was well known as a powerful seer to the network of treasure diggers . . . in western New York in the early 1800s."[321] As a result, many individuals approached Joseph for assistance. Martin Harris recorded an incident in 1827 when Joseph helped him find a lost pin with a seer stone.

> In the first place, he told me of this stone, and proposed to bind it on his eyes, and run a race with me in the woods. A few days after this, I was at the house of his father in Manchester, two miles south of Palmyra village, and was picking my teeth with a pin while sitting on the bars. The pin caught in my teeth, and dropped from my fingers into shavings and Northrop Sweet also did the same. We could not find it. I then took Joseph on surprise, and said to him—I said, "Take your stone." I had never seen it, and did not know that he had it with him. He had it in his pocket. He took it and placed it in his hat—the old white hat—and placed his face in his hat. I watched him closely to see that he did not look outside; he reached out his hand beyond me on the right, and moved a little stick, and there I saw the pin, which he picked up and gave to me. I know he did not look out of the hat until after he had picked up the pin.[322]

As Joseph Smith continued to associate with unscrupulous men in the business of treasure digging, he began to question whether God approved of his actions. Joseph Smith Sr. admitted in an 1826 trial—for disorderly conduct of an acquaintance—that both he and his son Joseph Jr. were mortified at the thought of Joseph's gift only being used for worldly purposes, like searching for filthy lucre. Joseph and his father offered up many prayers concerning his gift, asking that the Lord would make known his will.[323] They undoubtedly knew that the Lord had answered their prayers by September 1827. By this time, Moroni had appeared and instructed Joseph on numerous occasions concerning his gift and his future role as prophet, seer, revelator, and translator. Martin Harris stated that Moroni commanded Joseph, during one of his visits prior to receiving the plates, to "quit the company of the money-diggers; that there were wicked men among them" and that "he must have no more to do with them."[324] Regarding Joseph's early experience with magic and money-digging, and his preparation as a future leader of the restored Church, Bushman explained,

> When he married Emma Hale in 1827, Joseph was on the eve of realizing himself as a prophet. . . . Magic had served its purpose in his life. In a sense, it was a preparatory gospel. . . . After 1828, Joseph could no longer see that magic might have prepared him to believe in a revelation of gold plates and translation with a stone. It did not occur to him that without magic his family might have scoffed at his story of Moroni, as did the minister who rejected the First Vision. Magic had played its part and now could be cast aside.[325]

Translation of the Plates by Aid of the Divine Instruments

Three months after the Prophet Joseph received the plates and the Urim and Thummim, the translation commenced. From December 1827 to June 1828, Martin Harris acted as Joseph's scribe but was not permitted to continue in this capacity after losing the 116-page manuscript. Immediately following that setback, Moroni confiscated the plates and the Urim and Thummim from Joseph and did not return them until September 1828. During the next seven months after that point, Emma and John Whitmer served as scribes for Joseph, but progress was slow.[326] From April 7, 1829 to its completion in late June 1829, Oliver Cowdery assisted Joseph in the translation.[327]

Throughout the entire translation process, the Prophet Joseph used both the Urim and Thummim and a seer stone. Emma, in an interview with her son, described her experience with the translation project:

> In writing for your father I frequently wrote day after day, often sitting at the table close by him, he sitting with his face buried in his hat, with the stone in it, and dictating hour after hour with

> nothing between us. . . . He had neither manuscript nor book to read from. . . . If he had had anything of the kind he could not have concealed it from me. . . . Joseph could neither write nor dictate a coherent and well-worded letter, let alone dictate a book like the Book of Mormon. And, though I was an active participant in the scenes that transpired, and was present during the translation of the plates, and had cognizance of things as they transpired, it is marvelous to me, "a marvel and a wonder," as much so as to anyone else. . . . My belief is that the Book of Mormon is of divine authenticity—I have not the slightest doubt of it. I am satisfied that no man could have dictated the writing of the manuscripts unless he was inspired; for, when acting as his scribe, your father would dictate to me hour after hour; and when returning after meals, or after interruptions, he could at once begin where he had left off, without either seeing the manuscript or having any portion of it read to him. This was a usual thing for him to do. It would have been improbable that a learned man could do this; and, for one so ignorant and un-learned as he was, it was simply impossible.[328]

Emma mentioned that Joseph looked into the stone while his face was "buried in a hat." Some Latter-day Saints today are bothered by this practice, perhaps because it seems strange and they do not know how to interpret it. William Smith explained that the instruments "were much too large for Joseph and he could only see through one [of the stones] at a time—using sometimes one and sometimes the other. By putting his head in a hat or some dark object it was not necessary to close one eye while looking through the stone with the other. In that way sometimes when his eyes grew tired he relieved them of the strain."[329]

Apparently, while gazing into the stone, Joseph saw each word and even spelled out the difficult words. Emma reported that Joseph also saw, in the stones, what the scribe wrote down. "When my husband was translating the Book of Mormon," recalled Emma, "I wrote a part of it, as he dictated each sentence, word for word, and when he came to proper names he could not pronounce, or long words, he spelled them out, and while I was writing them, if I made a mistake in spelling, he would stop me and correct my spelling, although it was impossible for him to see how I was writing them down at the time."[330] Martin Harris reported that an entire sentence appeared in the stone that Joseph would subsequently read aloud. After writing the sentence, the scribe would say, "written." If the scribe penned the sentence incorrectly, it would remain visible to Joseph in the stone until it was properly translated and then a new sentence would appear.[331] These details correspond to a statement of David Whitmer.

> Sometimes Joseph could not pronounce the words correctly, having had but little education; and if by any means a mistake was made in the copy, the luminous writing would remain until it was corrected. It sometimes took Oliver several trials to get the right letters to spell correctly some of the more difficult words, but when he had written them correctly, the characters and the interpretation would disappear, and be replaced by other characters and their interpretation.[332]

Whitmer also recalled that when Joseph looked into the stone, a "spiritual light would shine" and "a piece of something resembling parchment would appear, and under it was the interpretation in English."[333] Joseph Knight stated that the English interpretation appeared in "Brite [*sic*] Roman Letters."[334]

Research conducted on the original manuscript of the Book of Mormon by Royal Skousen, a linguistics scholar, provides further details concerning what the Prophet Joseph may have seen while looking into the seer stone and the Urim and Thummim during the translation. Skousen discovered that Joseph probably saw at least twenty to thirty words at a time. We find an example of this in the original text of Alma 56:41, which Oliver translated as follows: "*& it came to pass that <we saw the Lamanites> when the light of the morning came we saw the Lamanites upon us.*" Regarding this example, Skousen explained,

> This example suggests that Joseph and Oliver started out together, but by the time Oliver finished writing "& it came to pass that" Joseph had moved along far enough that he was then dictating "we saw the Lamanites upon us" and Oliver started to write that

> down when he realized he had skipped the intervening text "when the light of the morning came," so he immediately crossed out "we saw the Lamanites" and wrote the correct sequence, possibly with Joseph repeating the correct text for him. If this explanation is correct, then it indicates that Joseph Smith had at least twenty words in view as he was dictating.[335]

Skousen's research, coupled with statements already mentioned, show that Joseph saw the spelling of difficult names in the stone. Two examples of this are found in the original manuscript of Alma 33:15 and Heleman 1:15.

> *"for it is not written that Zenos alone spake of these things but <Zenock> Zenoch also spake of these things;"*
>
> *"& they were lead by a man whose name was <Coriantummer> Coriantumr."*

Commenting on the latter passage, Skousen concluded,

> In this case, no matter how slowly or carefully Joseph Smith might have repronounced *Coriantumr*, it would have been impossible for him to have indicated that there was no vowel between the m and r at the end of the name except by actually spelling out the separate letters *m* and *r*. Nor could Oliver Cowdery have guessed this spelling since no word (or name) in English ends in *mr*. In fact, Oliver ends the correct spelling *Coriantumr* with a large flourish on the final *r*, which Oliver produces nowhere else in either the original or the printer's manuscript. This addition probably reveals Oliver Cowdery's frustration at having to guess at such a weird spelling.[336]

Skousen also discovered that Joseph probably saw in the instruments an indication to include a chapter break in the manuscript and that chapter numbers were not part of the original text. "Evidence," explained Skousen, "from both the original and printer's manuscripts show that Joseph Smith apparently saw some visual indication at the end of a section that the section was ending. . . . Recognizing [this], Joseph Smith then told the scribe to write the word chapter, with the understanding that the appropriate number would be added later." Skousen also explained that perhaps "the strongest evidence that the word chapter is not original to the revealed text is that the chapter numbers are assigned later in both manuscripts. The numbers are almost always written in heavier ink and more carefully." Concerning Skousen's research project in its entirety, he concluded,

> One of the interesting complexities of the original English-language text of the Book of Mormon is that it contains expressions that appear to be uncharacteristic of English in all of its dialects and historical stages. These structures also support the notion that Joseph Smith's translation is a literal one and not simply a reflection of either his own dialect or the style of early modern English found in the King James Version of the Bible. . . . All of this evidence (from the original manuscript, witnesses' statements, and from the text itself) is thus consistent with the hypothesis that Joseph Smith could actually see . . . the translated English text—word for word and letter for letter— and that he read off this revealed text to his scribe. . . . Evidence suggests that Joseph Smith was not the author of the Book of Mormon, not even its English language translation, although it was revealed spiritually through him and in his own language.[337]

Another significant account regarding the use of a seer stone during the translation process was provided by Martin Harris, who recounted the day when he replaced Joseph's stone with a fake.

> After continued translation, we would become weary, and would go down to the river and exercise by throwing stones out on the river, etc. While so doing on one occasion, I found a stone very much resembling the one used for translating, and on resuming our labor of translation, I put in place the stone that I had found. . . . The Prophet remained silent, unusually and intently gazing in darkness. . . . Much surprised, Joseph exclaimed, "Martin! What is the matter? All is as dark as Egypt!" My countenance betrayed me, and the Prophet asked me why I had done so. I said, "to stop the mouths of fools, who had told me that the Prophet had learned those sentences and was merely repeating them."[338]

Although Joseph and his scribes emphasized that God translated the plates through Joseph and the stones, they also mentioned that they were required to translate in the spirit of humility and righteousness. David Whitmer observed the following from his experience with Joseph and the translation:

> At times when brother Joseph would attempt to translate he would look into the hat in which the stone was placed . . . he found he was spiritually blind and could not translate. He told us that his mind dwelt too much on earthly things, and various causes would make him incapable of proceeding with the translation. When in this condition he would go out and pray, and when he became sufficiently humble before God, he could then proceed with the translation. . . . He was a religious and straight-forward man. He had to be; for he was illiterate and he could do nothing himself. He had to trust in God. He could not translate unless he was humble and possessed the right feelings towards everyone. To illustrate so you can see: One morning when he was getting ready to continue the translation, something went wrong about the house and he was put out about it. Something that Emma, his wife, had done. Oliver and I went upstairs and Joseph came up soon after to continue the translation but he could not do anything. He could not translate a single syllable. He went downstairs, out into the orchard, and made supplication to the Lord; was gone about an hour—came back to the house, and asked Emma's forgiveness and then came upstairs where we were and then the translation went on all right.[339]

There seems to be some confusion among many as to when Joseph used the Urim and Thummim as opposed to the seer stone during the translation process. Some accounts state that Joseph used the Urim and Thummim while other accounts claim Joseph used the seer stone. Concerning this matter, David Whitmer explained that Joseph used the Urim and Thummim and seer stone "alternately, as suited his convenience."[340] David most likely referred to the time before the 116-page manuscript was lost, as Emma recalled that "after that, [Joseph] used a small stone."[341] We also gather from statements of Martin Harris and David Whitmer that not only was the Urim and Thummim no longer used after the 116-page manuscript was lost, but neither was the gold plates. Martin Harris recalled that while the translation was in progress, "the plates would be on a table in the room in which Smith did the translating, covered over with a cloth."[342] Similarly, David Whitmer remembered that "when Joseph was again allowed to resume the translation, the plates were taken care of by a messenger of God."[343]

Although Joseph used the seer stone from September 1828 to June 1829, he also received several revelations via the Urim and Thummim. Moroni most likely kept the Urim and Thummim in his possession and only returned it to Joseph just long enough for him to receive a revelation. It does not appear that the Urim and Thummim was used following the organization of the Church in April 1830. Any statements made by the early brethren concerning its use after this date may be referring to the seer stone.[344]

Revelations and Visions through the Divine Instruments

Joseph most likely gazed into the Urim and Thummim for the first time in 1827 when Moroni told him to "look in the spectacles" to see who the Lord had prepared to assist with the translation. As Joseph looked, he "plainly" saw "Martin Harris, standing before him."[345] This was somewhat familiar to Joseph, as Moroni had previously commanded him to look into his seer stone to find out who should accompany him to the hill to obtain the plates.[346] In June 1828, nearly a year after Joseph looked into the Urim and Thummim for the first time, Martin pleaded with him to inquire of the Lord concerning the 116-page manuscript. Joseph related the following:

> Some time after Mr. Harris had begun to write for me, he began to importune me to give him liberty to carry the writings home and show them; and desired of me that I would inquire of the Lord, through the Urim and Thummim, if he might not do so. I did inquire, and the answer was that he must not. However, he was not satisfied with this answer, and desired that I should inquire again. I did so, and the answer was as before. Still he

> could not be contented, but insisted that I should inquire once more. After much solicitation I again inquired of the Lord, and permission was granted him to have the writings on certain conditions; which were, that he show them only to his brother, Preserved Harris, his own wife, his father and his mother, and a Mrs. Cobb, a sister to his wife.[347]

One month after losing the manuscript, Moroni appeared to Joseph and gave him the Urim and Thummim to receive instruction from the Lord. Joseph subsequently looked into the instrument and received a stern rebuke due to his carelessness.

> The works, and the designs, and the purposes of God cannot be frustrated. . . .
>
> For God doth not walk in crooked paths, neither doth he turn to the right hand nor to the left, neither doth he vary from that which he hath said, therefore his paths are straight, and his course is one eternal round. . . .
>
> Behold, you have been entrusted with these things, but how strict were your commandments; and remember also the promises which were made to you, if you did not transgress them. . . .
>
> For, behold, you should not have feared man more than God . . . Yet you should have been faithful. (D&C 3:1–2, 5 , 7–8)

Moroni appeared again in July 1828 with the Urim and Thummim and the Lord instructed Joseph on what he should translate next (see D&C 10). Nearly nine months later, in April 1829, he received another revelation by the Urim and Thummim directed to Oliver Cowdery. Evidently, he needed reassurance that the translation project was God's work. The revelation counseled Oliver to "be diligent; stand by my servant Joseph, faithfully, in whatsoever difficult circumstances he may be for the word's sake. . . . Did I not speak peace to your mind concerning the matter? What greater witness can you have than from God?" (D&C 6:18, 23 [14–23]).

Within a few weeks, Joseph and Oliver received another revelation through the Urim and Thummim regarding the Apostle John. "A difference of opinion," explained Joseph, "arising between us about the account of John the Apostle in the New Testament, as to whether he died or continued to live, we mutually agreed to settle it by the Urim and Thummim and the following is the word which we received."[348] The Lord informed them that the Apostle John desired to remain on the earth until his Second Coming as a "ministering angel" and that he shall "prophesy before nations, kindreds, tongues and people" (D&C 7:3, 6).

In May 1829, shortly after Joseph and Oliver received the Aaronic Priesthood, Joseph was given a revelation in the Urim and Thummim directed to Hyrum Smith. Joseph explained that "Hyrum Smith came to us to inquire concerning these things [baptism and Priesthood], when at his earnest request, I inquired of the Lord through the Urim and Thummim."[349] The Lord instructed Hyrum, among other things, to "study my word which hath gone forth among the children of men [Bible], and also study my word which shall come forth among the children of men, or that which is now translating [Book of Mormon]" (D&C 11:22).

A few days after Hyrum visited them in Harmony, Pennsylvania, Joseph and Oliver received further instruction from the Lord by the Urim and Thummim. One day while translating the plates Joseph "received instead of the words of the Book, a commandment to write a letter to David Whitmer . . . requesting him to come immediately with his team, and convey himself and Oliver to his own residence, as an evil-designing people were seeking to take away his (Joseph's) life."[350] David received the letter and traveled to Harmony in order to assist Joseph and Oliver. Before he left for Harmony, however, David was busy tending his crops when the letter arrived. "I did not know what to do," explained David, "I was pressed with my work. I had some 20 acres to plow."[351] Lucy Smith recorded that David had at least two days of work ahead of him and was not sure that he would be able to leave for Harmony. Oliver had become friends with the Whitmer family before meeting Joseph and frequently corresponded with David by letter. Lucy described the events that transpired after David received the letter.

> He then fastened his horses to the harrow, and instead of dividing the field into what is, by farmers, usually termed lands, drove around the whole of it, continuing thus till noon, when, on stopping for dinner, he looked around, and discovered to his surprise, that he had harrowed in full half the wheat. After dinner he went on as before, and by evening he finished the whole two days work. His father, on going into the field the same evening, saw what had been done, and he exclaimed, "There must be an overruling hand in this, and I think you would better go down to Pennsylvania as soon as your plaster of paris is sown."
>
> The next morning, David took a wooden measure under his arm and went out to sow the plaster, which he had left, two days previous, in heaps near his sister's house, but, on coming to the place, he discovered that it was gone! He then ran to his sister, and inquired of her if she knew what had become of it. Being surprised she said, "Why do you ask me? Was it not all sown yesterday?" "Not to my knowledge," answered David. "I am astonished at that," replied his sister, "for the children came to me in the forenoon, and begged of me to go out and see the men sow plaster in the field, saying, that they never saw anybody sow plaster so fast in their lives. I accordingly went, and saw three men at work in the field, as the children said, but, supposing that you had hired some help, on account of your hurry, I went immediately into the house, and gave the subject no further attention."[352]

David immediately began the one-hundred-mile journey to Harmony. Joseph had never met David prior to this meeting but saw him in the seer stone as he traveled. Upon arrival, Oliver told David that Joseph looked into the seer stone and knew the exact time of when David left Fayette, the towns in which he stopped in each day, and "even the name on the sign board of the hotel" he stayed the previous night. David was amazed upon hearing this, as Joseph's description of his journey was accurate.[353]

As the translation of the plates neared completion in June 1829, David, John, and Peter Whitmer Jr. approached Joseph and asked how they could assist in the Lord's work. Joseph recorded, "David, John and Peter Whitmer, Jun., became our zealous friends and assistants in the work; and being anxious to know their respective duties, and having desired with much earnestness that I inquire of the Lord concerning them, I did so, through the means of the Urim and Thummim" (see D&C 14, 15, and 16).[354] The Whitmer brothers were not the only individuals to approach Joseph in June of 1829 to request a revelation. Martin Harris, Oliver Cowdery, and David Whitmer, knowing that the Lord would soon allow three individuals to see Moroni and the plates, approached Joseph concerning the matter. Joseph recorded that they wanted him to "inquire of the Lord to know if they might not obtain of him the privilege to be these three special witnesses; and finally they became so very solicitous, and urged me so much to inquire that at length I complied."[355] The Lord revealed to them, through Joseph via the Urim and Thummim, that they would be the Three Witnesses (see D&C 17).

Joseph did not only use the Urim and Thummim and seer stones for the translation of the plates and for receiving revelations. In 1826, both Joseph Jr. and his father testified in court that while looking into the stones, Joseph "discovered that time, place and distance were annihilated; that all the intervening obstacles were removed, and that he possessed one of the attributes of Deity," namely, "an All-Seeing-Eye," meaning that he could see all things, past, present, and future.[356]

Concerning Joseph's ability to see all things in the Urim and Thummim, Lucy Smith stated that "it was by this that the angel showed [Joseph] many things which he saw in vision; by which also he could ascertain, at any time, the approach of danger, either to himself or the Record, and on account of which he always kept the Urim and Thummim about his person."[357] As an illustration, Lucy related one incident in 1827 when Joseph used the Urim and Thummim to check on the plates: "Just before Emma rode up to Mrs. Wells, Joseph from an impression that he had had, came up out of the well in which he was laboring and met [Emma] not far from the house. Emma immediately informed him of what had transpired, whereupon he looked in the Urim and Thummim and saw that the Record was . . . safe."[358]

Joseph not only saw things pertaining to the plates in the

stones, but David Whitmer stated that Joseph had "his entire past history revealed to him."[359] Joseph also saw the lives of many prominent martyrs in history. As mentioned previously, after reading the classic *Fox's Book of Martyrs,* Joseph wrote, "I have, by the aid of the Urim and Thummim [or seer stone], seen those martyrs, and they were honest, devoted followers of Christ, according to the light they possessed, and they will be saved."[360] Among the martyrs whom the Prophet Joseph saw were the New Testament apostles (see chapter 4), John Wycliffe, John Huss, Jerome of Prague, Martin Luther, William Tyndale, John Calvin, and John Wesley.

Perhaps the greatest vision and revelation that Joseph saw in either the Urim and Thummim or seer stone was the entire history of the Bible. Lorenzo Brown recalled Joseph saying on one occasion, "After I got through translating the Book of Mormon, I took up the Bible to read with the Urim and Thummim [or seer stone]. I read the first chapter of Genesis and I saw the things as they were done. I turned over the next and the next, and the whole passed before me like a grand panorama; and so on chapter after chapter until I read the whole of it. *I saw it all!*"[361] In addition, Joseph translated the Egyptian papyri with the seer stone and most likely saw that translation in a grand panorama as well. "The Lord is Blessing Joseph," Wilford Woodruff recorded in his journal dated February 19, 1842, "with Power to reveal the mysteries of the kingdom of God; to translate through the Urim and Thummim [or seer stone] Ancient records & Hyeroglyphics as old as Abraham or Adam."[362] Woodruff also explained that Joseph saw in vision, while translating the Book of Abraham, "Kolob, Oliblish, God sitting upon his throne, the earth, other planets, and many great and glorious things as revealed to Abraham through the power of the priesthood."[363] After analyzing all that Joseph saw in the Urim and Thummim and seer stones, we understand more fully his statement: "I have the whole plan of the kingdom before me and no other person has."[364]

The Urim and Thummim in the Eternities

In a meeting in April 1843 in Ramus, Illinois, Joseph taught,

> The angels do not reside on a planet like this earth; but they reside in the presence of God, on a globe like a sea of glass and fire, where all things for their glory are manifest—past, present, and future, and are continually before the Lord. The place where God resides is a great Urim and Thummim. This earth in its sanctified and immortal state, will be made like unto crystal and will be a Urim and Thummim to the inhabitants who dwell thereon, whereby all things pertaining to an inferior kingdom, or all kingdoms of a lower order, will be manifest to those who dwell on it; and this earth will be Christ's. Then the white stone mentioned in Revelation 2:17, will become a Urim and Thummim to each individual who receives one, whereby things pertaining to a higher order of kingdoms, will be made known; and a white stone is given to each of those who come into the Celestial Kingdom, whereon is a new name written, which no man knoweth save he that receiveth it. The new name is the key word.[365]

John the Revelator saw the sea of glass of heaven in vision: "And before the throne there was a sea of glass like unto crystal" (Revelation 4:6). Speaking of this sea of glass, Brigham Young taught, "This earth, when it becomes purified and sanctified, or celestialized, will become like a sea of glass; and a person, by looking into it, can know things past, present, and to come; though none but celestialized beings can enjoy this privilege. They will look into the earth, and the things they desire to know will be exhibited to them."[366] William Clayton commented on the connection between the Urim and Thummim and the "new name" as the "key word" mentioned above: "The grand key word was the first word Adam spoke and is a word of supplication. He [Joseph] found the word by the Urim and Thummim—it is that key word to which the heavens [are] opened."[367] In the Targum Pseudo-Jonathan of Exodus 28:30—an ancient Jewish Aramaic translation and commentary of the Bible—we find an interesting parallel as follows: "And you shall put into the breastplate the Urim, which illuminate their words and make manifest the hidden things of the House of Israel, and the Thummim which perfect their deeds, for the High Priest who seeks instruction from the Lord through them. Because *in them is engraved and exposed the great and holy Name by which the three hundred and ten worlds were created*."[368]

According to Joseph Smith, as well as certain Jewish legends, the Urim and Thummim and other sacred stones were used in the Creation and will be used by the righteous after they are resurrected. Friend of the Prophet, William W. Phelps, wrote a poem concerning the "stone" promised to the righteous in heaven mentioned in Revelation:

My Old White Stone

O keep my old "white stone," Father,
O keep it till I come;
The stone I had of thee at home,
Before this world was known;

For lo! in it is my "new name"—
The name thou gavest me,
When I was wash'd and set apart
For the glory yet to be.

Eternity is thine, Father,
Age after age has gone,
And yet, among thy sons, as one,
My spirit moves divine.

With light and life, and sense and love,
Through realms where wisdom's known,
To find, by faith, my path back home,
To my gem—my old "white stone."

The sweetest joy that seems, father,
Is now and then a view,
Of that eternal world and you,
That flashes through my dreams,
In some blest spot that's still and pure,
Where virtue's bliss is known,
And where my spirit eyes can see,
For themselves, my old "white stone."[369]

Conclusion

Joseph Smith's critics often claim that he fabricated the stories about these objects, and that they really did not operate as he claimed. Notice, however, that the overall portrayal of the Urim and Thummim and seer stones in early Latter-day Saint history, as presented in this chapter, is not posited conveniently and suspiciously in Joseph Smith's own journal; rather, the details of the nature of these instruments, as well as how Joseph operated them, is scattered among journals and writings of dozens of individuals associated with the Smith family. Moreover, it is clear from several accounts that the Urim and Thummim and seer stones were not the focus of the journals' authors but were mentioned in passing. That accounts describing Joseph Smith's use of the Urim and Thummim and seer stones seem to be congruous with ancient biblical and Jewish texts is amazing (and is expected among Latter-day Saints). Joseph used these ancient revelatory instruments on numerous occasions. He relied on them to translate the plates, to receive revelations from the Lord, and to see visions of past, present, and future events. These divinely sanctioned objects played a major role in the Restoration.

Chapter Six

Gathering the Saints

Naturally, people of faith wish to see visions and miracles in order to strengthen their belief. These types of experiences, however, are rare, even among early Latter-day Saint converts who were later called into the apostleship. Wilford Woodruff, for example, joined the Church when he discovered that the Mormons claimed guidance by prophets and apostles, exactly what he was searching for.[370] Brigham Young joined the Church following several years of studying the doctrines because of what he felt while listening to the simple testimony of another man.[371] Orson Pratt, Parley Pratt, and Willard Richards all joined due to the effect that the Book of Mormon had on them. John Taylor joined after hearing Parley Pratt preach concerning various aspects of the Church.[372] Hundreds of accounts exist that are similar to these, of people who were baptized because of what they felt as they "investigated" Mormon scripture and teachings.

This chapter focuses, however, on the accounts of several early converts who joined the Church due to miraculous experiences: visions, healings, and other heavenly manifestations. Although these types of experiences are rare, they played a major role in the Restoration. Just as the Lord needed Joseph Smith to use revelatory instruments (Urim and Thummim and seer stones) early in his prophetic career in order to push along the work, the Lord also needed to bring people into the restored Church at a rapid pace, and he used manifestations to accomplish it. The following accounts further illustrate the role that heavenly manifestations played in the early decades of the Church.

Early Converts

Ezra Booth and Mr. and Mrs. Johnson

In 1831, an incident occurred in the Smith home that led to the baptism of at least three individuals. Ezra Booth, a Methodist preacher of Mantua, Ohio, accompanied his wife, Elsa Johnson, her husband, and others to the Smith home in Hiram, Ohio. They went to visit with the Prophet Joseph about his newly established church. During the discussion, the topic turned to spiritual gifts that were demonstrated in the days of the New Testament apostles. Someone in the group commented on the condition of Elsa Johnson—who had been afflicted for many years with rheumatism and was unable to lift her arm—saying, "Here is Mrs. Johnson with a lame arm; has God given any power to man now on the earth to cure her?" Soon after, when the conversation had turned to another topic, the Prophet Joseph stood and walked across the room to where Elsa was seated and taking her by the hand said in the most "impressive manner," "Woman, in the name of the Lord Jesus Christ I command thee to be whole." He immediately exited the room, leaving the company to marvel at what they had just witnessed. Elsa suddenly lifted her arm and the company rejoiced at the miracle they had witnessed. Elsa returned home and was able to perform tasks that she had been unable to do for a long time. Because of this miracle, Ezra Booth, as well as Mr. and Mrs. Johnson, requested that the Prophet Joseph baptize them.[373]

Benjamin Brown

In the late 1820s and early 1830s, Benjamin Brown searched for a church that claimed the same organization and authority that existed in the "ancient Church." "I was a person," stated Brown, "that thought much about the things of God and often . . . asked myself this question: where is the people of God?" Shortly after meeting the missionaries in the fall of 1832, Brown considered seriously joining the Church and began reading the Book of Mormon.[374] Brown related a remarkable experience he received one day while praying about the Book of Mormon.

> I took the Book [of Mormon] and laid it before the Lord, and pleaded with him in prayer for a testimony whether it was true or false, and, as I found it stated that the Three Nephites had power to show themselves to any persons they might wish, Jews or Gentiles, I asked the Lord to allow me to see them for a witness and testimony of the truth of the Book of Mormon, and I covenanted with him, if he complied with my request, that I would preach it even at the expense of my life, should it be necessary.
>
> The Lord heard my prayer, and, about five days after, two of the three visited me in my bedroom. I did not see them come, but I found them there. One spoke to me for some time, and reproved me sharply on account of my behavior at the time when I first attended the meeting of the Saints, and treated so lightly the gift of tongues. He told me never, as long as I lived, to do so again, for I had grieved the Spirit of the Lord, by whose power that gift had been given. This personage spoke in the Nephite language, but I understood, by the Spirit which accompanied him, every word as plainly as if he had spoken in English. I recognized the language to be the same as that in which I had heard Father Fisher speak at the meeting. Such a rebuke, with such power, I never had in my life before or since, and never wish to have again. I was dumb before my rebuker, for I knew that what he said was right, and I felt deserving of it. How these men went, I do not know, but directly they were gone, the Spirit of the Lord said to me, "Now, you know for yourself! You have seen and heard! If you now fall away, there is no forgiveness for you."[375]

Zebedee Coltrin

Zebedee Coltrin, a Methodist of Strongsville, Ohio, encountered Latter-day Saint missionaries and began investigating the Church. On January 8, 1831, Coltrin heard a sermon of Solomon

Hancock. Coltrin returned home following the sermon and "lay meditating" upon what he heard. "The room," recalled Coltrin, "became lighted up with a brilliant light and I saw a number of men dressed in white robes."[376] The next day Coltrin requested baptism. He remained a faithful member of the Church his entire life and was ordained to the First Council of the Seventy in 1835.

Jonathan Crosby

Jonathan Crosby, a good friend of the Prophet Joseph, helped expand the young Church. Crosby spent many hours with the brethren studying Hebrew and attending the School of the Prophets.[377] In 1833, before joining the Church, Crosby had a dream shortly after becoming affiliated with the Methodist Church.

> I dreamed that some new preachers came with a book containing new doctrine, and which threw new light on the Bible, and their preaching was different from that of all others and that I rejoiced in it. But when I awoke the dream somewhat left me, and I thought no more about it. The next Sabbath after I was propounded, I went to meeting again and it being quite early, I went into a store kept by two young men and they told me that two young men, preachers, had come to town, had put up at the tavern, and would preach in the hall that evening; that they had a new book, a record, which had been found, and was an addition to the Bible. "Well," I said, "I am glad of it. I hope they have got the truth. I can't see the propriety of so much division in the world about religion. I shall go and hear them."[378]

Crosby attended the meeting and heard sermons on the Book of Mormon. The following day, missionaries stopped by Crosby's home and conversed with him about the sermons. Crosby suggested that they accompany him to his Methodist preacher's home and have a discussion about religion. Crosby explained what transpired following their arrival.

> This Mr. Harris was tending his mill. I introduced them and Mr. Harris took the Mormon book, looked it over a moment, asked some questions about it which they answered; also in regard to

> the ordinances of the gospel, particularly baptism, which they also answered. He then stopped his mill and invited us into the house. After we were seated, he conversed awhile with them, but entered into no argument with them, at which I marveled. And I said to him sometime afterward, "I brought those men to you for you to whip them out in argument." He replied, "They have the truth, and I can't do it, neither can anyone." "Well, I did not believe you could, but I wanted them tested." I knew it, their preaching was true, and I rejoiced exceedingly.[379]

Homer Duncan

In July 1831, fifteen-year-old Homer Duncan of Barnet, Vermont, heard someone read passages from the Book of Mormon. Duncan was convinced of its truthfulness and began pondering what he had heard. Duncan then saw a vision that he described as follows:

> Between twelve and one o'clock, noon, while in my bedroom, my eyes were opened so that I could see far away to the west. As I looked, I saw two Elders coming to our place, who, when they arrived, said, "We have new manna from heaven, just sent down." They further said that they were sowing it broadcast over the earth, and every person who partook of it, and who continued to do so, would be saved, while those that rejected it would be damned. Many partook of it, some liking it and others turning away from it. Of those that partook were my father, who was a Congregationalist deacon, Hazen Aldrich, a Methodist class leader, Daniel S. Miles, a Universalist, and Orson Johnson, an atheist. I saw them baptized on the 15th day of May, 1832, and I saw that I would be plowing in the field that day. I also saw that Hazen Aldrich would apostatize, and that I would join the Church after that. I likewise saw my brother Chapman go to the western States to be baptized. This was the end of the vision.

Duncan, however, was not baptized immediately. A year later in 1832, he met Orson Pratt and Lyman E. Johnson whom he recognized from his vision. Duncan saw them baptize the three other men from his vision on May 15, 1832. Duncan stated, "I was also ploughing in the fields on that day, as I had seen in the vision. My brother was baptized in 1832, in Jackson County, Missouri. Hazen Aldrich apostatized during the winter of 1837–38, and I was baptized in Grand River, at Adam-Ondi-Ahman, Missouri, in 1838."[380]

Oliver Granger

In 1830, Moroni visited Oliver Granger after he read the recently published Book of Mormon. Sarah Granger Kimball, the daughter of Oliver, stated that the heavenly visitation led to her father's conversion to Mormonism. Sarah related, "My father was told by a person who said his name was Moroni that the Book of Mormon, about which his mind was exercised, was a true record of great worth." Moroni instructed Oliver to continually testify of the truthfulness of the Book of Mormon and if he did so faithfully, he "should hereafter be ordained to preach the everlasting Gospel to the children of men." Moroni also instructed Oliver to kneel and offer a prayer. As he prayed, "Moroni and another personage knelt with him by the bedside. Moroni repeated words and instructed [Oliver] to repeat them after him."[381]

Edward Hunter

In 1839, Edward Hunter of Newtown, Pennsylvania, had an experience that led to his conversion. Hunter traveled a few miles one night to hear a Latter-day Saint elder preach. Upon arrival, Hunter heard that the young missionary was in danger of being attacked by men who opposed the Church. Upon meeting Elder Elijah H. Davis, Hunter observed that "he was a humble young man." Hunter listened to his sermon but could not pay enough attention as he worried over his safety. Hunter related,

> I was sitting by Dr. Griffith, our representative. Robert Johnson, one of the trustees, addressing the Elder, said: "I wish you would say something about the Atonement." He spoke well on the subject, but before he was through Johnson interrupted him and ordered him to quit preaching. I sprang up and said: "He is a stranger and shall have justice shown him and be respected; we

> will hear him and then hear you speak." I was informed that there were many present opposed to the "Mormons," but I resolved as I lived that Mr. Davis should be protected, if I had to meet the rabble on their own ground. I kept my eye on them and determined to stand by him at the risk of person and property. I had friends, though Mr. Davis had none. Mr. J. Johnson, brother to Robert Johnson, came to me as I was going out and apologized for his brother's conduct. I walked out of the crowd, got on my horse and rode home alone.

Hunter retired to bed but could not sleep as he lay pondering the events of the day. "My reflections were," recalled Hunter, "why have I taken such a decided stand for those strangers, and I asked the Lord: 'Are those Mormons thy servants?' Instantly, a light came in the room at the top of the door, so great that I could not endure it." Shortly following this experience, Hunter received a personal visit from Joseph Smith. Hunter was baptized a short time later on October 8, 1840, by Elder Orson Hyde who was en route to Jerusalem to dedicate the Holy Land for the return of the Jews. Edward Hunter remained faithful in the Church and was ordained to be the Presiding Bishop in 1851.[382]

Heber C. Kimball and Others

Heber C. Kimball, future apostle in the Church and counselor in the First Presidency, along with a Methodist preacher, John P. Greene, John Young Sr., and others, saw a vision while living in Mendon, New York, on the night of September 22, 1827.

> I had retired to bed, when John P. Greene, who was living within a hundred steps of my house, came and waked me up, calling upon me to come out and behold the scenery in the heavens. I woke up and called my wife and Sister Fanny Young (sister to Brigham Young), who was living with us, and we went out-of-doors. It was one of the most beautiful starlight nights, so clear that we could see to pick up a pin. We looked to the eastern horizon, and beheld a white smoke arise toward the heavens; as it ascended it formed itself into a belt, and made a noise like the sound of a mighty wind, and continued southwest, forming a regular bow dipping in the western horizon. After the bow had formed, it began to

Heber C. Kimball

widen out and grow clear and transparent, of a bluish cast; it grew wide enough to contain twelve men abreast.

In this bow an army moved, commencing from the east and marching to the west; they continued marching until they reached the western horizon. They moved in platoons, and walked so close that the rear ranks trod in the steps of their file leaders, until the whole bow was literally crowded with soldiers. We could distinctly see the muskets, bayonets and knapsacks of the men, who wore caps and feathers like those used by the American soldiers in the last war with Britain; and also saw their officers with their swords and equipage, and the clashing and jingling of their implements of war, and could discover the forms and features of the men. The most profound order existed throughout the entire army; when the foremost man stepped, every man stepped at the same time; I could hear the steps. When the front rank reached the western horizon a battle ensued, as we could distinctly hear the report of arms and the rush.

No man could judge of my feelings when I beheld that army of men, as plainly as ever I saw armies of men in the flesh; it seemed as though every hair of my head was alive. This scenery we gazed upon for hours, until it began to disappear.

After I became acquainted with Mormonism, I learned that this took place the same evening that Joseph Smith received the records of the Book of Mormon from the angel Moroni, who had held those records in his possession. John Young, Sen., and John P. Greene's wife, Rhoda, were also witnesses. My wife, being frightened at what she saw, said, "Father Young, what does all this mean?" "Why, it's one of the signs of the coming of the Son of Man," he replied, in a lively, pleased manner. The next night similar scenery was beheld in the west by the neighbors, representing armies of men who were engaged in battle.[383]

A few years later, many of those who witnessed the vision in the sky encountered the elders of the Church. One day after attending a meeting where the missionaries spoke, Heber C. Kimball and others saw another vision that persuaded them to join the Church.

> Father John Young, Brigham Young, Joseph Young and myself had come together to get up some wood for Phineas H. Young. While we were thus engaged we were pondering upon those things which had been told us by the Elders, and upon the saints gathering to Zion, when the glory of God shone upon us, and we saw the gathering of the saints to Zion, and the glory that would rest upon them; and many more things connected with that great event, such as the sufferings and persecutions that would come upon the people of God, and the calamities and judgments that would come upon the world. These things caused such great joy to spring up in our bosoms that we were hardly able to contain ourselves, and we did shout aloud "Hosannah to God and the Lamb."[384]

Heber and many individuals from the Young family, including Brigham, joined the Church shortly thereafter and remained strong members their entire lives.

Abigail Leonard

Abigail Leonard recorded three visions she saw that prepared her for the Restoration.

> In 1829, Eleazer Miller came to my house, for the purpose of holding up to us the light of the gospel, and to teach us the necessity of a change of heart. He did not teach creedism, for he did not believe therein. That night was a sleepless one to me, for all night long I saw before me our Savior nailed to the cross. I had not yet received remission of my sins, and, in consequence thereof, was much distressed. These feelings continued for several days, till one day, while walking alone in the street, I received the light of the spirit.
>
> Not long after this, several associated Methodists stopped at our house, and in the morning, while I was preparing breakfast, they were conversing upon the subject of church matters, and the

best places for church organization. From the jottings of their conversation, which I caught from time to time, I saw that they cared more for the fleece than the flock. The Bible lay on the table near by, and as I passed I occasionally read a few words until I was impressed with the question: "What is it that separates two Christians?" For two or three weeks this question was constantly on my mind, and I read the Bible and prayed that this question might be answered to me.

One morning I took my Bible and went to the woods, when I fell upon my knees, and exclaimed: "Now, Lord, I pray for the answer of this question, and I shall never rise till you reveal to me what it is that separates two Christians." Immediately *a vision passed before my eyes, and the different sects passed one after another by me, and a voice called to me, saying: "These are built up for gain."* Then, beyond, I could see a great light, and a voice from above called out: *"I shall raise up a people, whom I shall delight to own and bless."* I was then fully satisfied, and returned to the house.

Not long after this a meeting was held at our house, during which every one was invited to speak; and when opportunity presented, I arose and said: "Today I come out from all names, sects and parties, and take upon myself the name of Christ, resolved to wear it to the end of my days."

For several days afterward, many people came from different denominations and endeavored to persuade me to join their respective churches. At length the associated Methodists sent their presiding elder to our house to preach, in the hope that I might be converted. While the elder was discoursing I beheld a vision in which *I saw a great multitude of people in the distance, and over their heads hung a thick, dark cloud. Now and then one of the multitude would struggle, and rise up through the gloomy cloud; but the moment his head rose into the light above, the minister would strike him a blow, which would compel him to retire; and I said in my heart, "They will never serve me so."*

Not long after this, I heard of the Book of Mormon . . . I requested that I might know of the truth of this book, by the gift and power of the Holy Ghost, and I immediately felt its presence. Then, when the Book of Mormon came, we were ready to receive it and its truths. The brethren gathered at our house to read it, and such days of rejoicing and thanksgiving I never saw before nor since. We were now ready for baptism, and on or about the 20th of August, 1831, were baptized.[385]

Alexander and Ellen Neibaur

Having been born and raised in France into a Jewish family, Alexander Neibaur, to the dismay of his parents who urged him to become a rabbi, chose to pursue a career in dentistry. Following his graduation from the University of Berlin, Neibaur converted to Christianity and moved to Preston, England. In 1837, a few years following his arrival, twenty-nine-year-old Neibaur had a dream in which he saw a book that possessed truth concerning salvation. One morning, shortly following his dream, he and his wife, Ellen, were cleaning their house when a neighbor within shouting distance called out, "Have you seen the new ministers from America?" "No," replied Ellen, who was standing on the front porch. "Well," continued the neighbor, "they claim to have seen an angel." "What?" Neibaur yelled with much excitement as he ran to the window. "What is that you say?" When the information was repeated, he inquired as to where he could find these American missionaries. Neibaur found Elders Heber C. Kimball, Willard Richards, Orson Hyde, and others who recently arrived in England on July 30, 1837. Neibaur immediately asked the missionaries if they had a book other than the Bible in their possession, to which they answered affirmatively as they presented him with a copy of the Book of Mormon. As soon as he saw the book, he instantly recognized it from the book in his dream. Three days later, after reading the Book of Mormon from cover to cover, Neibaur requested baptism. The missionaries recommended that he study the doctrines further to be sure he was prepared, to which Neibaur replied, "Gentlemen, I am prepared."

Although Neibaur felt ready, he postponed his baptism until the next spring as he waited for his wife, who felt unsure about the Church and the Book of Mormon, calling it a "pretty story." Elder Isaac Russell baptized Neibaur on April 9, 1838. Ellen, however, was still unsure and decided not to follow her husband and be baptized. A short time later, Ellen requested baptism after seeing, in a dream, the face of Elder Willard Richards formed in the clouds and felt that it was a sign telling her to investigate the Church more seriously. She was baptized shortly thereafter. Three years later in February 1841, Alexander and Ellen Neibaur traveled to Nauvoo, Illinois. Shortly following their arrival, Alexander established his own dentistry practice, assisted in building the Nauvoo Temple, and tutored the Prophet Joseph in Hebrew and German.[386]

Sarah Pea

Sarah Pea, a Methodist of Looking-Glass Prairie, Illinois, recorded a dream that she had of two Mormon missionaries.

> In the summer of 1835 two Mormon elders came to preach at my father's house by request of my father, as he had met them in the town of Belleville, nine miles from my father's house. I, together with my father and mother were at that time members of the Reformed Methodist Church. The two elders came and held a meeting and preached on the first principles of the gospel, and related to the people about there being a prophet in their church, and told us about the Book of Mormon, and about an angel appearing to the prophet and others; all of which was new doctrine to the people, so as it was in the afternoon they held their meeting, my father invited them to stop all night, which invitation they accepted as they were then on their way to Kirtland, Ohio, some five hundred miles from where we then lived. So after supper was over a number of neighbors gathered in to hear these strangers talk, but I felt anxious to see the Book of Mormon they had told us about and I asked one of the elders if I could see the book and read some in it that evening. So he gladly handed me the book, and I asked the company to excuse me for the evening and most of the night I spent in reading that book. I truly was greatly astonished at its contents that it left an impression upon my mind not to be forgotten—for in fact the book appeared to be open before my eyes for weeks but the next morning those men bid us goodbye and started on their journey for Ohio. So our family had many things to say about this strange people; but still the things they told us left a deep impression on our minds, not easy to be forgotten.
>
> But yet we did not think of ever meeting with those strange men again; and after they had been gone six weeks, I had a dream

> concerning them. I dreamed on a Friday night that they would come to our house the next evening just as the sun would be setting, and they would first come in sight at the end of a long lane in front of our house. I also dreamed that I met them on the porch and of the remark that was made both by them and of the remark made by myself, which I will relate later on.
>
> So in the morning father and mother were going to Belleville, a town nine miles away, and while we were at breakfast I asked my father if he would not try to come home early that evening. He answered, "Why are you so particular, is your young man coming?" I said, "No, father, but those two Mormon elders will be here tonight." "Why," said my father, "have you heard from them?" I said, "No, but I dreamed last night that they would be here, and I feel sure it will be so." Father said I must be crazy for those men were hundreds of miles away. I said, "Father, hurry home this evening for I am sure they will come." He only laughed at me, and he and mother went off to town. Then said my sister, "Let us prepare for those men for they will surely be here." She too, laughed at me, but as it was Saturday we went to work baking and preparing for Sunday, as that was our custom to do on Saturday; and as the day passed on I began to look once in awhile down the lane for those men.
>
> Sure enough, just as the sun was setting they made their appearance just where I dreamed I first saw them. I met them on the porch, and bid them the time of day by saying, "I have been looking for you to come." "Why," said they, "had you heard we were coming?" "No," said I, "but I dreamed last night that you were coming and I felt sure you would be here." "Well," said one of the elders, "and we had a vision that we were to return here and baptize you and build up a Church in this region." I said, "Well, that is something for the future," but bid them to take chairs and be comfortable for my father and mother drove into the yard and as I was standing on the porch my father said to me, "Well, Sarah, where are your Mormon elders?" I told him they were in the house, at the same time they stepped out onto the porch to meet my father, who seemed struck with astonishment remembering what I told him in the morning about my dream.[387]

Sarah and her family eventually joined the Church. Later in her life, Sarah married Charles C. Rich, a devoted man who accepted many assignments given to him by the Prophet Joseph, including presiding over a branch of the Church at Mount Pisgah, Iowa.

Zera Pulsipher

Zera Pulsipher, a Baptist minister of Onondaga, New York, witnessed an experience in 1811 that prepared him for the message that the Latter-day Saint missionaries would deliver to him twenty years later. When Zera was twenty-two years old, his wife appeared to him after she died. Zera said that she looked "pleasant as she ever did." His wife sat by his side and assisted him in singing a hymn. Zera said that the first words of the hymn were, "That glorious day is drawing nigh when Zion's Light Shall Shine." The vision eased his anxiety regarding her "condition in the spirit world . . . as she seemed to enjoy herself well." The hymn taught Zera of a "great work of the last dispensation of the fullness of times." Twenty years later, Zera related an experience after encountering the Mormon missionaries and the Book of Mormon.

> In the fall of 1831 there was a Book of Mormon brought in to town. I succeeded in getting it. I directly read it through twice, gave it a thorough investigation, and believed it was true and the winter following Jared Carter came that was from a mission to Vermont or Lake George. As soon as he came into town I, with two Methodist Preachers went to see him after a reasonable introduction I questioned him upon the principles of the ancient gospel with all its gifts belonging to it. I asked him if he believed it, he answered in the affirmative. I asked him if he had ever laid hands on the sick and they had recovered. Yes, he said, he had in many instances.
>
> He preached the following evening to a crowded congregation, held up the Book of Mormon and declared it to be a revelation from God. I could not gainsay anything he had said, he sat down and gave liberty for remarks, the congregation seemed to be in a maze not knowing what to think of what they had heard. I arose and said to the congregation that we had been hearing strange things and if true they were of the utmost importance to us. If not true it was one of the greatest impositions and as the

> preacher had said that he had got his knowledge from heaven and was nothing but a man and I the same, that I had just as good a right to obtain that blessing as he, therefore I was determined to have that knowledge for myself which I considered it my privilege, from that time I made it a matter of fervent prayer.
>
> I think about the seventh day as I was thrashing in my barn with doors shut, all at once there seemed to be a ray of light from heaven which caused me to stop work for a short time, but soon began it again. Then in a few minutes another light came over my head which caused me to look up. I thought I saw the angels with the Book of Mormon in their hands in the attitude of showing it to me and saying "this is the great revelation of the last days in which all things spoken of by the prophets must be fulfilled." The vision was so open and plain that I began to rejoice exceedingly so that I walked the length of my barn crying "Glory Hal-la-lu-ya to the God and the Lamb forever."[388]

Zera remained faithful to the Church throughout his life and was ordained to the First Council of the Seventy on March 6, 1838.

Ezra Thayre

In October 1830, thirty-nine-year-old Ezra Thayre of Randolph, Vermont, attended a meeting where Hyrum Smith preached. Thayre related the incident.

> When Hyrum began to speak, every word touched me to the inmost soul. I thought every word was pointed to me. God punished me and riveted me to the spot. I could not help myself. The tears rolled down my cheeks, I was very proud and stubborn. There were many there who knew me, I dare not look up. I sat until I recovered myself before I dare look up. They sung some hymns and that filled me with the Spirit. When Hyrum got through, he picked up a book and said, "Here is the Book of Mormon." I said, let me see it. I then opened the book, and I received a shock with such exquisite joy that no pen can write and no tongue can express. I shut the book and said, "What is the price of it?" "Fourteen shillings" was the reply. I said, I'll take the book. I opened it again, and I felt a double portion of the Spirit, that I did not know whether I was in the world or not. I felt as

> though I was truly in heaven. Martin Harris rushed to me to tell me that the book was true. I told him that he need not tell me that, for I knew that it is true as well as he. . . . I withdrew from the company . . . and sat down alone.

As Ezra pondered over the events of the day, "a rainbow came down on each side of the room." Ezra heard a voice say, "You have done well. . . . I am God that made heaven and earth, and there is none other God beside me." Ezra then saw a man appear, whom he later discovered was Oliver Cowdery, and present him with a document and a trumpet. Oliver told Ezra to blow the trumpet, to which Ezra replied, "I never blowed any in my life." Oliver encouraged him to try it. "I put it in my mouth and blowed on it," related Ezra, "and it made the most beautiful sound that I ever heard." Ezra also stated that the document was a "revelation on me and Northrop Sweet." Ezra saw many other things in vision. A week later, Ezra met the Prophet for the first time, related his vision to him, and said that he knew the Book of Mormon was true. Joseph asked him what was hindering him from being baptized. Ezra replied, "I am ready and willing at any time." Ezra related,

> We started to the water, which was four or five miles off. When I got on the way I saw the same horses and the same persons, (6 of them) that I saw in the before mentioned vision, and the houses all along were the same as had been shown me. When I came to the grist mill, I saw that I had seen it in the vision, but I had never been there before. We were baptized just below the mill. There was a green meadow which I had seen before. Parley P. Pratt baptized us, as I had seen him in the vision. I saw him pull two fish out of the water and another which was a small fish. I saw that I and Oliver's mother were the two persons referred to in the vision. The small fish meant Northrop Sweet. He was baptized at the same time, but soon left the church.

Shortly following Ezra's baptism, Joseph Smith received a revelation in which the Lord told him that Ezra and Northrop Sweet were to go on a mission and "lift up" their "voices as with the sound of a trump, to declare my gospel unto a crooked and perverse generation" (D&C 33:2). Ezra realized that this was the revelation given to him by Oliver in vision shortly before his baptism.[389]

John Young

In April 1832, following their first encounters with the missionaries, Joseph and Phineas Young, brothers of Brigham Young, traveled to Pennsylvania to visit a small branch of the Church. While visiting, Joseph was baptized and ordained an elder. Joseph subsequently traveled to New York and Canada to preach the gospel to his family and friends. John chastised his brother, saying, "Joseph, you have received a new doctrine, and another spirit from what you have had heretofore, and I fear it is a delusion; for the scriptures say that many false spirits have gone out into the world, and this is one of them." Shortly thereafter, John, suffering from pains in his head, "threw himself on the hearth." While laying in this condition, he requested a blessing from Joseph, saying, "You profess to have the priesthood of an institution that heals the sick. If you have received such a gift as that, I wish you would lay your hands on me." Joseph agreed and then proceeded to lay his hands upon John's head and subsequently blessed him. Moments later, John was "perfectly healed." Because of this experience, John agreed to consider the Mormon Church with an open mind. A few months later, John was baptized by his brother Joseph.[390]

Wandle Mace, Theodore Curtis, and Others

While Parley P. Pratt was preaching at a meeting in New York City in 1837, a woman approached him and said, "I had a dream of you and of the new Church the other night."[391] Concerning this woman, Parley wrote, "I have also been to visit . . . [the] lady who believes. And the Lord had shown [her] in a dream concerning me. [She] saw me in a dream. She had been seeking to find God's people. . . . As soon as she heard me preach and read the Book of Mormon she said she believed it all."[392] Shortly thereafter, the woman was baptized.

Parley also related the healings of five people in New York City, which resulted in at least eight baptisms. The first woman, who had been in the care of a doctor for four years because of a crippled leg, arose and walked immediately after being blessed by Parley and his companion, Elder Elijah Fordham. The doctor, having witnessed the healing, became angry and threatened to sue the missionaries. The other woman was also blessed and immediately arose and walked after being confined to her bed for many years with a "dumb palsy." Parley described the last three healings in New York City as follows:

> A child of Mr. Wandle Mace, of No. 13 Bedford street, was healed of brain fever in the last stage, when the doctors had given it over, and the kindred and neighbors had gathered in to see it die. I laid my hands on it, in the presence of them all, and it was healed, and in a few hours took nourishment, and commenced to play and run about the floor. In the same house, in an upper chamber, lay a woman, by the name of Dexter, sick, who had not left her room, nor scarcely her bed, for some six months; she was at the point of death, and her babe also, who had taken the disease from her. Her mother, who had the care of her, was present when the child was healed, and she ran upstairs and told the woman that there were men below who healed the sick, as in days of old, by the laying on of hands in the name of Jesus. The woman exclaimed: "Thank God, then I can be healed." She sent for us, and was from that hour restored to health, and the child also. She walked about two miles to the East River and was baptized, and then walked home again—it being a very wet day with snow and rain, and the sidewalks about shoe deep in snow and mud. After these three miracles of healing had been witnessed in that house in Bedford street, six persons who witnessed them were baptized, viz: Wandle Mace and wife, Theodore Curtis and wife, and the sick woman and her mother, before named.[393]

Conclusion

As illustrated by the accounts cited above, visions and miracles played a major role in bringing many people into Christ's Church in the early days of the Restoration. Thousands of people have recorded similar miracles that influenced them in joining the Church. Ancient prophets prophesied that miracles would accompany the last days just before the return of the Messiah. Ancient rabbis and well-known Christians also believed that visions, dreams, and miracles would accompany God's kingdom in the last days. We should not be surprised, then, that the Lord poured out manifestations upon an entire generation to prepare the way for the establishment of His Church in the latter days. These manifestations acted as a catalyst for the Restoration. Without them, the restored gospel may not have taken hold at worst and may have developed extremely slow at best.

Endnotes

Chapter 1

1. Joseph Smith, *History of the Church of Jesus Christ of Latter-day Saints* (Salt Lake City: Deseret Book, 1948), 1:2–3.
2. See Gordon Wood, "Evangelical America and Early Mormonism," *New York History* 61 (1980): 381.
3. See William L. Stone, *Matthias and His Impostures: Or, the Progress of Fanaticism* (New York: Harper & Brothers, 1835).
4. Douglas L. Winiarski, "Souls Filled with Ravishing Transport: Heavenly Visions and the Radical Awakening in New England," *The William and Mary Quarterly*. 61, no. 1 (January 2004): 10.
5. Ibid., 26.
6. See Susan Juster, *Doomsayers: Anglo-American Prophecy in the Age of Revolution* (Philadelphia: University of Pennsylvania Press, 2003).
7. Ann Kirschner, "'Tending to Edify, Astonish, and Instruct,' Published Narratives of Spiritual Dreams and Visions in the Early Republic," *Early American Studies* 1, no. 1 (Spring 2003).
8. *Millennial Star* 10 (Oct. 1848): 302–3.
9. *History of the Church*, 1:15.
10. Joseph Sr. and Lucy would have also been aware of Asael Smith's prediction. Asael, the grandfather of Joseph Smith Jr., felt that there would be a prophet raised up in his family. Concerning this matter, the Prophet Joseph wrote, "My grandfather, Asael Smith, long ago predicted that there would be a prophet raised up in his family, and

my grandmother was fully satisfied that it was fulfilled in me. My grandfather Asael died in East Stockholm, St. Lawrence county, New York, after having received the Book of Mormon, and read it nearly through; and he declared that I was the very Prophet that he had long known would come in his family" (*History of the Church*, 2:443).

11. Joseph Smith, *The Personal Writings of Joseph Smith*, ed. Dean C. Jessee (Salt Lake City: Deseret Book, 1984), 199–201.

12. *History of the Church*, 4:536.

13. *History of the Church*, 1:4–5.

14. Lucy Mack Smith, *The History of Joseph Smith by His Mother* (American Fork, UT: Covenant Communications, 2000), 82.

15. It was mentioned that Joseph Smith Sr. did not particularly like Rev. Benjamin Stockton of the Presbyterian Church. This same man told the congregation during Alvin's funeral sermon that he "had gone to hell, for Alvin was not a church member." Interview with William Smith by E. C. Briggs and J. W. Peterson, published in the Deseret News, 20 January 1894; see also Lavina F. Anderson, ed., *Lucy's Book: A Critical Edition of Lucy Mack Smith's Family Memoir* (Salt Lake City: Signature Books, 2001), 332.

16. *Personal Writings of Joseph Smith*, 1:443, 444.

17. Orson Hyde, *Ein Ruf aus der Wüste* (A Cry out of the Wilderness), 1842, extract, English translation, retrieved from http://josephsmithpapers.org/paperSummary/orson-hyde-ein-ruf-aus-der-wste-a-cry-out-of-the-wilderness-1842-extract-english-translation.

18. Joseph Smith Papers, Journal, 1835–1836, November 9, 1835, retrieved from, http://josephsmithpapers.org/paperSummary/journal-1835-1836#!/paperSummary/journal-1835-1836&p=24

19. *History of the Church*, 1:5.

20. *Personal Writings of Joseph Smith*, 1:7.

21. *Times and Seasons*, (November 1841–October 1842), 3, no. 9 (March 1, 1842), 706–7; spelling and punctuation changed for readability.

22. *Joseph Smith, History, [ca. June 1839–ca. 1841]; handwriting of James Mullholland and Robert B. Thomson; sixty-one pages; in Joseph Smith History, 1838–1856, vol. A-1, CHL,* retrieved from, http://josephsmithpapers.org/paperSummary/

history-circa-june-1839-circa-1841-draft-2?p=2#!/paperSummary/history-circa-june-1839-circa-1841-draft-2&p=3; spelling and punctuation changed for readability.

23. Winiarski, "Souls Filled with Ravishing Transport," 6. Some spelling changed for readability.

24. Ibid., 7.

25. Delivered in February 17, 1856, *Journal of Discourses* (Liverpool: F. D. and S. W. Richards, 1854–86), 3:205–6.

26. Winiarski, "Souls Filled with Ravishing Transport," 10; emphasis added.

27. Ibid., 18; emphasis added.

28. John F. Firth, *The Experience and Gospel Labours of the Rev. Benjamin Abbott* (Philadelphia: D&S, 1825), 6–7, 10, 13–14, emphasis added.

29. John H. Wigger, *Taking Heaven by Storm: Methodism and the Rise of Popular Christianity in America* (New York: Oxford University Press, 1998), 113–14.

30. Bernard A. Weisberger, *They Gathered at the River: The Story of the Great Revivalists and Their Impact upon Religion in America* (Chicago: Quadrangle Books, 1966), 47; emphasis added.

31. Robert V. Remini, *Joseph Smith* (New York: Viking Penguin, 2002), 10.

32. Caleb Rich, "A Narrative of Elder Caleb Rich," *Candid Examiner*, 2 (April 30–June 18, 1827): 179–96, 205–8.

33. Elias Smith, *The Life, Conversion, Preaching, Travels, and Sufferings of Elias Smith* (Portsmouth, NH: Beck & Foster, 1816), 59.

34. Nathan Culver, *A Very Remarkable Account of the Vision of Nathan Culver, late of Newton, New York: Sewing His Deistical and Vicious Principles, and How He was Converted to the Truth, by an Extraordinary and Immediate Revelation, Jan. 10, 1791* (Portsmouth, NH: Oracle Office, 1796).

35. Sarah Alley, *Account of a Trance or Vision of Sarah Alley, of Beekman Town, Dutchess County, State of New-York, Which happened on First-day Evening, the Twenty-fifth of Second Month 1798, taken from her own Mouth, the Twenty-Seventh of the same Month, in the Hearing of divers Persons* (Philadelphia: n.p.), 1807.

36. Orson F. Whitney, *The Life of Heber C. Kimball*, Collector's Edition (Salt Lake City: Bookcraft, 1992), 94.

37. Truman Madsen, *Joseph Smith the Prophet* (Salt Lake City: Bookcraft, 1989), 12.

38. *A Wonderful Account of a Little Girl of nine years old, Who lives in the Town of Jericho, in the State of Vermont; by the Name of Hannah Coy* (Windsor, VT: n.p., 1800); emphasis added; see also Ann Kirschner, *Early American Studies*, 198, 203, 207.

39. Nathan Barlow, *A Vision Seen By Nathan Barlow, of Freetown (Called so by the Inhabitants) Adjacent to the North End of Harlem, in the County of Kennebec, District of Maine.* January 8, 1801 (Greenfield, MA: n.p., 1802); emphasis added.

40. *The Religious Experience of Norris Stearns, Written by Divine Command, Shewing the Marvellous Dealings of God to His Soul, and the Miraculous Manner in which He Was Delivered from the Jaws of Death and Hell; and His Soul Set at Liberty, Likewise His Appointment to the Ministry; and Commision from on High, to Preach the Gospel to Every Creature* (Greenfield, MA: 1815); emphasis added.

41. Charles G. Finney, *Memoirs of Rev. Charles G. Finney. Written by Himself* (New York: Barnes, 1876), 19–20; emphasis added.

42. Joseph Smith Jr., *Teachings of the Prophet Joseph Smith*, comp. Joseph Fielding Smith (Salt Lake City: Deseret Book, 1976), 181.

43. Richard L. Saunders, "The Fruit of the Branch: Francis Gladden Bishop and His Culture of Dissent," in *Differing Visions: Dissenters in Mormon History*, ed. Roger D. Launius and Linda Thatcher (Urbana, IL: University of Illinois Press, 1994), 102–4, 106, 109.

44. Billy Hibbard, *Memoirs of the Life and Travels of B. Hibbard, Minister of the Gospel* (New York: Piercy & Reed, 1843), 6–7, 23–25; emphasis added.

45. Journal of John Murdock, 1792–1864, typescript, Archive and Manuscripts, Harold B. Lee Library, Brigham Young University, 3.

Chapter 2

46. Joseph Smith, *The Personal Writings of Joseph Smith*, ed. Dean C. Jessee (Salt Lake City: Deseret Book, 1984), 199–204.

47. Joseph Smith Jr., *History of the Church of Jesus Christ of Latter-day Saints*, ed. B. H. Roberts. 2nd ed., rev. (Salt Lake City: The Church of Jesus Christ of Latter-day Saints, 1976), 5:517.

48. *Personal Writings of Joseph Smith*, 347.

49. *History of the Church*, 3:303–304.

50. Stephen E. Robinson, *Are Mormons Christians?* (Salt Lake City: Bookcraft, 1991), 35.

51. Tad R. Callister, *The Inevitable Apostasy, and the Promised Restoration* (Salt Lake City: Deseret Book, 2006), 290–91.

52. David W. Bercot, *Will The Real Heretics Please Stand Up: A New Look At Today's Evangelical Church in the Light of Early Christianity* (Tyler, TX: Scroll, 1999), 149.

53. William Tyndale and John Frith, *The Works of the English Reformers: William Tyndale and John Frith*, ed. Thomas Russell (London: n.p., 1831), 1:403.

54. John Wesley, *The Works of John Wesley*, ed. Frank Baker et al. (Oxford: Clarendon, 1975), 7:26–27.

55. Ibid., vol. 2, sermon 66; emphasis added.

56. Roger Williams, *Bloody Tenent Yet More Bloody*, 203; as quoted in C. Leonard Allen, "Roger Williams and 'the Restauration of Zion,'" in *The American Quest for the Primitive Church*, ed. Richard Hughes, (Urbana: University of Illinois Press, 1988), 42.

57. William Cullen Bryant, ed., *Picturesque America, or the Land We Live In* (New York: Appleton, 1894), 502; emphasis added.

58. Pierre Van Paassen, *A Crown of Fire: The Life and Times of Girolamo Savonarola* (New York: Charles Scribner's Sons, 1960), 172.

59. *The Universalist Leader* (Universalist Publishing House, 1925), 28:296.

60. Ralph Waldo Emerson, *The Complete Essays and Other Writings of Ralph Waldo Emerson*, ed. Brooks Atkinson (New York: Modern Library, 1940), 75, 71, 80.

61. Carl H. Sederholm, "A Tale of Two Smiths: Joseph Smith, Elias Smith, and God's Great Work of Salvation" in *Archive of Restoration Culture: Summer Fellows' Papers 1997–1999* (Provo, UT: Joseph Fielding Smith Institute of Latter-day Saint History, 2000) 89–92, 96.

62. Bercot, *Real Heretics*, 151; emphasis added.

63. Alexander Campbell, *The Christian System: In Reference to the Union of Christians, and a Restoration of Primitive Christianity, as Plead in the Current Reformation* (Cincinnati: Standard Publishing, 1839), 250; emphasis added.

64. Alexander Campbell, *The Christian Baptist* (Cincinnati: Burnet, 1835), 5:402. Emphasis added.

65. Richard Hughes, "Joseph Smith as an American Restorationist," in *The Worlds of Joseph Smith*, ed. John W. Welch (Provo, UT: Brigham Young University Press, 2006),,34.

66. Elizabeth Goodliffe, "Joseph Smith and John Humphrey Noyes: Two Millennialists' Views on Economics and Marriage," in *Archive of Restoration Culture: Summer Fellows' Papers 1997–1999* (Provo, UT: Joseph Fielding Smith Institute of Latter-day Saint History, 2000), 71–72; Hughes, "Joseph Smith as an American Restorationist," 35–36; emphasis added.

67. Ludwig Pastor, *History of the Popes, from the Close of the Middle Ages* (St. Louis: Herder, 1898), 14:134.

68. Francis A. Sullivan, *From Apostles to Bishops: The Development of the Episcopacy in the Early Church* (New York: Newman Press, 2001), 15–16. Emphasis added.

69. LeGrand Richards, *A Marvelous Work and a Wonder* (Salt Lake City: Deseret Book, 1976), 3; emphasis added.

70. Charles W. Upham, *The Life of Timothy Pickering* (Boston: Little, Brown, 1878), 327–28.

71. Albert E. Bergh, *The Writings of Thomas Jefferson* (Washington, DC: Thomas Jefferson Memorial Association, 1907), 15:391; emphasis added.

72. Ibid., 15:288; emphasis added.

73. Thomas Jefferson, "A Bundle of Thomas Jefferson's Letters," in *Publications of the Buffalo Historical Society,* ed. Frank H. Severance (Buffalo, NY: Buffalo Historical Society, 1904), 7:28; emphasis added.

74. See Irving Wallace et al., "Hebrew: National Language of the U.S.," *Parade Magazine* (May 30, 1982): 16.

75. Hughes, "Joseph Smith as an American Restorationist," 36.

76. Hughes, "Joseph Smith as an American Restorationist," 37.

77. *Latter-day Saints' Messenger and Advocate* 3 (November 1836): 404.

78. Perry Miller, "The Old Testament in Colonial America," in *Historical Viewpoints*, ed. John A. Garraty (New York: Harper and Row, 1970), 1–95.

79. John W. Nevin, "Antichrist and the Sect System," in James Hastings Nichols, ed., *The Mercersburg Theology* (New York: n.p., 1966), 93–119.

80. See Joshua William Brooks, *A Dictionary of Writers on the Prophecies, with the Titles and Occasional Descriptions of their Works* (London: Simpkin, Marshall, 1835).

81. *Times & Seasons*, 6 (January 15, 1845--February 15, 1846): 858–59; see also JST Revelation 12.

82. Alonzo L. Gaskill, *The Lost Language of Symbolism* (Salt Lake City: Deseret Book, 2003), 117–19.

83. Thomas Hodgkin, *Italy and Her Invaders* (Oxford: Clarendon, 1880), 215–18.

84. See Merrill Unger, *Unger's Bible Dictionary* (Chicago: Moody, 1961), 68; Dr. Francis Nigel Lee, "The Anti-Preterist Historicism of John Calvin and the Westminster Standards" (2000), *Reformation Bookshelf* CD, "Sovereignty of God in History" (Still Waters Revival Books, 2003); *The Panoplist and Missionary Magazine* (Boston: Farrand, Mallory, 1809), 1:36; James Barmby, *Gregory the Great* (London: Society for Promoting Christian Knowledge, 1892), 206.

85. Lee, "Anti-Preterist Historicism"; emphasis added.

86. *Adam Clarke's Commentary on the Bible*, abr. Ralph Earle (Grand Rapids, MI: Baker, 1967), commentary on Revelation 12:15–16.

87. Edward Bishop Elliott, *Horae Apocalypticae* (London: Seeley, Burnside, and Seeley, 1847), 137; emphasis added.

88. Rev. John Dowling, *The History of Romanism: from the Earliest Corruptions of Christianity to the Present Time* (New York: Edward Walker, 1845), 57.

89. *Panoplist and Missionary Magazine*, 36. Emphasis added.

90. Philip Allwood, *A Key to the Revelation of St. John the Divine* (London: Rivington, 1829), 1:xvi, xvii; emphasis added.

91. Martin Luther, *Familiar Discourses* (London: Printed for W. Heptinstal, 1791), 7–8. Emphasis added.

92. William Ward, *The Fulfilment of Revelation; or Prophetic History of the Declensions and Restoration of the Christian Church* (London: M'Dowall, 1810–1820), 5:31, 68, 242; as cited in Daniel MacGregor, *A Marvelous Work and a Wonder; The Gospel Restored*

(1923; repr., Independence, MO: Board of Publications Church of Christ [Temple Lot], 1971), 90–91.

93. Ward, *Prophetic History*, 5:74, as cited in MacGregor, *Marvelous Work*, 91.

94. Errett Gates, *The Disciple of Christ* (New York: Baker & Taylor, 1905), 176.

95. W. H. Oliver, *Prophets and Millennialists: The Uses of Biblical Prophecy in England from the 1790s to the 1840s* (Auckland: Auckland University Press, 1978), 98.

96. *Times & Seasons*, 5 (January 1844–January 1, 1845): 732.

97. *Times & Seasons*, 6 (January 15, 1845–February 15, 1846): 858–59; emphasis added.

98. Robert Norton, *The Restoration of Apostles and Prophets In the Catholic Apostolic Church* (N.p.: Bosworth & Harrison, 1861), 15–18.

99. Samuel Davis, *Sermons on Important Subjects* (Boston: Lincoln and Edmands, 1810), 34.

100. Oliver, *Prophets and Millennialists*, 16–17.

101. William Cuninghame, *A Dissertation on the Seals and Trumpets of the Apocalypse and the Prophetical Period of 1260 years* (London: Thomas Cadell, 1843), 443; as cited in Smith, *Daniel and the Revelation*, 640.

102. Robert Reid, *The Seven Last Plagues or the Vials of the Wrath of God: a Treatise on the Prophecies in Two Parts* (Pittsburgh: Maclean, 1828), 44, 176–78.

103. Caleb Rich, "A Narrative of Elder Caleb Rich," *Candid Examiner*, 2 (April 30–June 18, 1827), 179–96, 205–8; see also Stephen A. Martini, *Radical Sects of Revolutionary New England* (N.p.: Harvard University Press, 1982), 72–74; emphasis added.

104. Cowley, *Wilford Woodruff*, 16–17; Wilford Woodruff, *Leaves From My Journal* (American Fork, UT: Covenant Communications, 2005), 2–4; emphasis added. Speaking of Robert Mason, Wilford Woodruff said, "The first opportunity I had after the truth of baptism for the dead was revealed, I went forth and was baptized for him in the temple font at Nauvoo. He was a good man, a true prophet; for his prophecies have been fulfilled. There was so much reason in the teachings of this man, and such harmony between

them and the prophecies and teachings of Christ and of the apostles and prophets of old, that I believed in them with all my heart" (Cowley, *Wilford Woodruff,* 18).

105. Chloe Willey, *A Short Account of the Life and Remarkable View of Mrs. Chloe Willey, of Goshen, N.H.* (New York: Totten, 1810), 21–22.

106. Several accounts in Latter-day Saint history describe individuals being raised from the dead. See, for example, Parley P. Pratt, *Autobiography of Parley P. Pratt,* ed. Scot F. Proctor and Maurine J. Proctor (Salt Lake City: Deseret Book, 2000, 355; Levi Curtis, "Recollections of the Prophet Joseph Smith," *Juvenile Instructor* 27, no. 12 (15 June 1892): 385–86; Oliver B. Huntington, "History of the Life of Oliver B. Huntington, Written by Himself 1878-1990," typescript, Special Collections, Harold B. Lee Library, Brigham Young University, Provo, UT, 53; Cowley, *Wilford Woodruff,* 97–98.

107. Larry E. Dahl and Donald Q. Cannon, *Encyclopedia of Joseph Smith's Teachings* (Salt Lake City: Bookcraft, 1997), 154.

108. For the description of many of these visions see Lucy Mack Smith, *The History of Joseph Smith by His Mother* (American Fork, UT: Covenant Communications, 2000), 68–73, 297–98.

109. Lavina F. Anderson, ed. *Lucy's Book: A Critical Edition of Lucy Mack Smith's Family Memoir* (Salt Lake City: Signature Books, 2001), 295–96; emphasis added.

110. Ibid.

111. *The Religious Experience of Norris Stearns, Written by Divine Command, Shewing the Marvellous Dealings of God to His Soul, and the Miraculous Manner in which He Was Delivered from the Jaws of Death and Hell; and His Soul Set at Liberty, Likewise His Appointment to the Ministry; and Commision from on High, to Preach the Gospel to Every Creature* (Greenfield, MA: n.p. 1815); emphasis added.

112. Solomon Chamberlain, "Short Sketch of the Life of Solomon Chamberlain, Written 11 July 1858," LDS Church Archives; see also Larry C. Porter, "Solomon Chamberlain-Early Missionary," *BYU Studies* 12 (Spring 1972): 314–18.

113. *Classic Experiences and Adventures* (Salt Lake City: Bookcraft, 1969), pt. 3, 22-23; emphasis added.

114. Ibid., 26; emphasis added.

115. Andrew Jenson, *Latter-day Saints Biographical Encyclopedia* (Salt Lake City: Andrew Jenson History, 1901), 1:224; emphasis added.

116. Elizabeth Whitney, "A Left from an Autobiography," *Woman's Exponent*, Sept. 1, 1878, 51.

117. *History of The Church*, 4:42.

118. *History of The Church*, 5:499.

119. "Remarkable Vision and Revelation; as seen by Asa Wild, of Amsterdam, N.Y.," *Wayne Sentinel*, 1, no. 4, (22 October 1823); emphasis added. For further analysis of Wild's publication, see Elden J. Watson, "The 'Prognostication' of Asa Wild," *BYU Studies* 37, no. 3 (1997–1998): 223–30.

120. William Cuninghame, *A Dissertation on the Seals and Trumpets of the Apocalypse and the Prophetical Period of 1260 years* (London: Cadell, 1843), 282.

121. John Taylor, *The Gospel Kingdom: Selections from the Writings and Discourses of John Taylor*, sel., arr., and ed., G. Homer Durham, (Salt Lake City: Deseret Book, 1943), 2–3.

122. Richard L. Bushman, "The Visionary World of Joseph Smith," *BYU Studies* 37, no. 1 (1997–1998): 192.

123. Robert V. Remini, *Joseph Smith* (New York: Viking Penguin, 2002), 6.

Chapter 3

124. "Autobiographical Sketch of Jos. Bates Noble," Mormon Biography File, LDS Church Archives, Salt Lake City, Utah.

125. See H. Donl Peterson, "Moroni: Joseph Smith's Tutor," *Ensign* 22 (January 1992): 22–29. Alexander L. Baugh discusses a few of these manifestations in detail and briefly mentions the others in "Documented Visions of Joseph Smith," in *Opening the Heavens: Accounts of Divine Manifestations 1820–1844*, ed. John W. Welch (Salt Lake City: Deseret Book and Provo, UT: Brigham Young University Press, 2005), 307–11.

126. Moroni appeared to Joseph in Nauvoo and instructed him regarding temple clothing (see Matthew B. Brown, *The Gate of Heaven* (American Fork, UT: Covenant Communication, 1999), 316.

127. *Journal of Discourses* (Liverpool: Richards and Richards, 1854–86), 6:368.

128. *Ante-Nicene Christian Library: Translations of the Writings of the Fathers Down to A.D. 325*, ed. Alexander Roberts and James Donaldson (Edinburgh: T. and T. Clark, 1867), 220; emphasis added.

129. *Journal of Discourses*, 23:362.

130. *Times and Seasons*, 3, no. 9 (November 1841–October 1842): 706–7.

131. Joseph Smith, *The Personal Writings of Joseph Smith*, ed. Dean C. Jessee (Salt Lake City: Deseret Book, 1984), 202–3.

132. *Personal Writings of Joseph Smith*, 213–14.

133. *Latter-day Saints' Messenger and Advocate*, 1, no. 5 (October 1834–September 1835): 79.

134. *Kansas City Times*, April 11, 1895.

135. *Personal Writings of Joseph Smith*, 213–14.

136. *Personal Writings of Joseph Smith*, 204.

137. Joseph Smith Jr., *History of the Church of Jesus Christ of Latter-day Saints*, ed. B. H. Roberts. 2nd ed., rev. (Salt Lake City: The Church of Jesus Christ of Latter-day Saints, 1976), 1:11–12.

138. *Latter-day Saints' Messenger and Advocate*, 1, no. 5, (February 1835): 80.

139. *Personal Writings of Joseph Smith*, 203–4; *Latter-day Saints' Messenger and Advocate*, 1, no. 5 (February 1835): 79–80; *Latter-day Saints' Messenger and Advocate*, 1, no. 7 (April 1835): 109–112.

140. *History of the Church*, 1:13–14.

141. Lucy Mack Smith, *The History of Joseph Smith by His Mother* (American Fork, UT: Covenant Communications, 2000), 88.

142. *History of the Church*, 1:14–15; Lucy Mack Smith also recorded the incident as follows: "The next day, my husband, Alvin, and Joseph, were reaping together in the field, and as they were reaping, Joseph stopped quite suddenly, and seemed to be in a very deep study. Alvin, observing it, hurried him, saying, 'We must not slacken our hands or we will not be able to complete our task.' Upon this Joseph went to work again, and after laboring a short time, he stopped just as he had done before. This being quite unusual and strange, it attracted the attention of his father, upon which he discovered that Joseph was very pale. My husband, supposing that he was sick, told him to go to the house, and have his mother doctor him. He

accordingly ceased his work, and started, but on coming to a beautiful green, under an apple tree, he stopped and lay down, for he was so weak he could proceed no further. He was here but a short time, when the messenger whom he saw the previous night, visited him again, and the first thing he said was, 'Why did you not tell your father that which I commanded you to tell him?' Joseph replied, 'I was afraid my father would not believe me.' The angel rejoined, 'He will believe every word you say to him.' Joseph then promised the angel that he would do as he had been commanded. Upon this, the messenger departed, and Joseph returned to the field, where he had left my husband and Alvin; but when he got there, his father had just gone to the house, as he was somewhat unwell. Joseph then desired Alvin to go straightway and see his father, and inform him that he had something of great importance to communicate to him, and that he wanted him to come out into the field where they were at work. Alvin did as he was requested, and when my husband got there Joseph related to him all that had passed between him and the angel the previous night and that morning. Having heard this account, his father charged him not to fail in attending strictly to the instruction which he had received from this heavenly messenger. Soon after Joseph had this conversation with his father, he repaired to the place where the plates were deposited." Lavina F. Anderson, ed. *Lucy's Book: A Critical Edition of Lucy Mack Smith's Family Memoir* (Salt Lake City: Signature Books, 2001), 339–40.

143. *Times & Seasons*, 3, no. 13 (November 1841–October 1842): 772.

144. Letter of James A. Briggs in *Cleveland Leader*, 37 (January 19, 1884).

145. Anderson, ed. *Lucy's Book*, 347.

146. *Latter-day Saints' Messenger and Advocate*, 2, no. 13 (October 1835–September 1836): 198.

147. *Latter-day Saints' Messenger and Advocate*, 2, no. 13 (October 1835–September 1836): 200.

148. Lucy Smith, *History of Joseph Smith by His Mother*, 86–87.

149. Anderson, ed. *Lucy's Book*, 345–47.

150. *Personal Writings of Joseph Smith*, 207.

151. Lucy Smith, *History of Joseph Smith by His Mother*, 103–4.

152. *History of the Church*, 1:16.

153. Lucy Smith, *History of Joseph Smith by His Mother*, 111.

154. See *Times & Seasons*, 3, no. 14 (16 May 1842): 785.

155. Lucy Smith, *History of Joseph Smith by His Mother*, 132.

156. *Personal Writings of Joseph Smith*, 210.

157. Lucy Mack Smith records what Joseph related to her after he received the plates on September 22, 1828: "After the angel left me . . . I continued my supplications to God, without cessation, and on the twenty-second of September, I had the joy and satisfaction of again receiving the Urim and Thummim, with which I have again commenced translating, and Emma writes for me, but the angel said that the Lord would send me a scribe, and I trust his promise will be verified. The angel seemed pleased with me when he gave me back the Urim and Thummim, and he told me that the Lord loved me, for my faithfulness and humility." Anderson, ed. *Lucy's Book*, 428.

158. Lucy Smith, *History of Joseph Smith by His Mother*, 135–38; *History of the Church*, 1:32.

159. *The Anchor Bible Dictionary*, ed. David Noel Freedman (New York: Doubleday, 1992), 1:816–19.

160. See Hayyim Schauss, *The Jewish Festivals* (New York: Schocken Books, 1938), 170–207.

161. Edward Chumney, *The Seven Festivals of the Messiah* (Shippensburg, PA: Treasure House, 1994), 181.

162. Ibid., 181, 193–94; emphasis added.

163. Kevin J. Conner, *Interpreting the Symbols and Types* (Portland, OR: City Bible Publishing, 1992), 179; see also Alonzo L. Gaskill, *The Lost Language of Symbolism: An Essential Guide for Recognizing and Interpreting Symbols of the Gospel* (Salt Lake City: Deseret Book, 2003), 323.

164. The autumn equinox falls on approximately September 22 every year; however, occasionally it will fall on the early morning of September 23.

165. Gaskill, *Language of Symbolism*, 150–56.

166. See Lenet H. Read, "Joseph Smith's Receipt of the Plates and the Israelite Feast of Trumpets," *Journal of Book of Mormon Studies* 2, no. 2 (Fall 1993).

167. Chumney, *Seven Festivals*, 107–9.

168. See Anderson, ed. *Lucy's Book*, 428.

169. B. H. Roberts, *Life of John Taylor* (Salt Lake City: Cannon & Sons, 1892), 27–28.

170. Roberts, *Life of John Taylor*, 27–28; emphasis added.

171. Orson F. Whitney, *The Life of Heber C. Kimball*, collector's ed. (Salt Lake City: Bookcraft, 1992), 442.

172. *Journal of Discourses*, 16:266.

173. *Journal of Discourses*, 17:374.

174. *Journal of Discourses*, 13:47.

175. Helen Mar Whitney, *A Woman's View: Helen Mar Whitney's Reminiscences of Early Church History*, ed. Jeni Broberg Holzapfel & Richard Neitzel Holzapfel (Provo, UT: Religious Studies Center, Brigham Young University, 1997), 173.

176. *Woman's Exponent*, 10, no. 18, February 15, 1882, 138.

177. Robert V. Remini, "Biographical Reflections on the American Joseph Smith," in *The Worlds of Joseph Smith*, ed. John W. Welch (Provo, UT: Brigham Young University Press, 2006), 27.

178. Hugh B. Brown, Conference Report, October 1958, 62.

179. Gordon Wood, "Evangelical America and Early Mormonism," *New York History* 61 (1980): 381; emphasis added.

180. Richard T. Hughes, "Joseph Smith as an American Restorationist," in *The Worlds of Joseph Smith*, 38–39.

181. *History of the Church*, 1:39–41.

182. Ibid., 3:29.

183. *Personal Writings of Joseph Smith*, 421.

184. Milton V. Backman Jr., *Eye-Witness Accounts of the Restoration* (Salt Lake City: Deseret Book, 1986), 112. Backman combined this statement from the "1832 History" and the "1842 History."

185. *History of the Church,* 1:238.

186. *Journal of Discourses*, 17:374.

187. *History of the Church*, 1:245.

188. N.B. Lundwall, *The Vision or The Degrees of Glory* (Salt Lake City: Bookcraft, 1948), 11.

189. *Juvenile Instructor*, 27, May 15, 1892, 303–4.

190. Philo Dibble (autobiography, 1806–c. 1843), "Early Scenes in Church History," in *Four Faith Promoting Classics* (Salt Lake City: Bookcraft, 1968), 81.

191. *History of the Church*, 1:252–53.

192. Joseph Smith Jr., *Teachings of the Prophet Joseph Smith*, comp. Joseph Fielding Smith (Salt Lake City: Deseret Book, 1976), 304.

193. *Journal of Discourses*, 20:70.

194. See chapter heading of Doctrine and Covenants 76 in the current LDS edition.

195. Wilford Woodruff, *The Discourses of Wilford Woodruff*, ed. G. Homer Durham (Salt Lake City: Bookcraft, 1946), 29.

196. "Martha Cragun Cox (1852-1932) Autobiography, 1928-1930." LDS Church Archives; as cited in Mark McConkie, ed., *Remembering Joseph: Personal Recollections of Those Who Knew the Prophet Joseph Smith* (Salt Lake City: Deseret Book, 2003), 210–11.

197. Doctrine and Covenants 110:11–16.

198. *History of the Church*, 3:388.

199. *Journal of Discourses*, 21:94.

200. *History of the Church*, 5:347.

201. "Diary of Oliver B. Huntington, 1847–1900," pt. 2, 207.

202. Daniel Tyler, "Recollections of the Prophet Joseph Smith," *Juvenile Instructor*, 27, 1892, 93.

203. Coltrin Zebedee, "High Priest Minutes, Spanish Fork, Utah, February 5, 1870," Archives of the Church of Jesus Christ of Latter-day Saints, Salt Lake City, Utah.

204. Whitney, *Life of Heber C. Kimball*, 91–92.

205. *History of the Church*, 2:427.

206. Whitney, *Life of Heber C. Kimball*, 91.

207. *Journal of Discourses* (Liverpool: F. D. and S. W. Richards, 1854-86), 11:10.

208. *Latter-day Saints' Messenger and Advocate*, 1 (February 1835), no. 5, 79.

209. Gaskill, *Language of Symbolism*, 74. See Exodus 39:27.

210. *Journal of Discourses*, 9: 376.

211. Truman Angell, Autobiography, Our Pioneer Heritage, BYU Special Collections, 198; See also BYU Studies, 15, no. 4 (1974–1975): 550–51.

212. *History of he Church*, 2:427.

213. *Journal of Discourses*, 11:10.

214. A. Karl Larson and Katharine Miles Larson, eds. *Diary of Charles Lowell Walker* (Logan, UT: Utah State University Press, 1980), 2:563.

215. Fred C. Collier and William S. Harwell, *Kirtland Council Minute Book* (Salt Lake City: Collier's, 1996), 29–38. Originally published in the *Kirtland Council Minute Book* housed in the LDS Church Archives in Salt Lake City, UT.

216. Ora Haven Barlow, *The Israel Barlow Story and Mormon Mores* (Salt Lake City: Publishers Press, 1968), 113–14.

217. Edward Stevenson, *Reminiscences of Joseph, the Prophet, and the Coming Forth of the Book of Mormon* (Salt Lake City: n.p., 1893), 6.

218. See any edition of *Fox's Book of Martyrs.*

Chapter 4

219. See *Deseret Evening News*, January 20, 1891.

220. Lucy Mack Smith, *The History of Joseph Smith by His Mother* (American Fork, UT: Covenant Communications, 2000), 109–10.

221. Katharine Smith Salisbury interview with her grandson, H. S. Salisbury, August 31, 1854, 2.

222. Lavina F. Anderson, ed., *Lucy's Book: A Critical Edition of Lucy Mack Smith's Family Memoir* (Salt Lake City: Signature Books, 2001), 387–88.

223. William Smith, "William B. Smith's Last Statement," *Zion's Ensign*, January 13, 1894, 6.

224. William Smith, "Sermon in the Saints' Chapel," Deloit, Iowa, June 8, 1884, *Saints' Herald* 31 (1884): 643-44.

225. Letter of Katharine Smith Salisbury, March 10, 1886, *Saints' Herald* 33 (1886): 260.

226. Anderson, ed. *Lucy's Book*, 390.

227. Sally Parker to Francis Tufts, August 26, 1838, document in possession of a descendent of Katharine Smith, as cited in Richard L. Anderson, *Investigating the Book of Mormon Witnesses* (Salt Lake City: Deseret Book, 1981), 25.

228. Letter of Martha L. Campbell to Joseph Smith Jr., December 19, 1843, "Josiah Stowell Papers," located in LDS Church Historian's office, as cited in B. H. Roberts, *A Comprehensive History of The Church of Jesus Christ of Latter-day Saints* (Provo, UT: Brigham Young University Press, 1965), 1:98.

229. "Last testimony of Sister Emma," *Saints' Herald* 26 (October 1, 1879): 289–90.

230. Joseph B. Noble, Autobiographical Sketch, 1810–1836, LDS Church Archives.

231. Lucy Smith, *History of Joseph Smith by His Mother*, 114.

232. *Tiffany's Monthly*, 5, no. 4, August 1859, 167.

233. Statement of David B. Dille, September 15, 1853, MS 21 (August 20, 1859): 545–46.

234. Lucy Smith, *History of Joseph Smith by His Mother*, 117–18.

235. Ibid., 121.

236. "Interview with Martin Harris," *Tiffany's Monthly*, May 1859, 169.

237. *Journal of Discourses* (Liverpool: Richards and Richards, 1854–86), 7:164.

238. Andrew Jenson. *Latter-day Saints Biographical Encyclopedia* (Salt Lake City: Andrew Jenson History, 1901), 1:283; sketch of David Whitmer and Peter Whitmer, *Historical Record*, 7, 621.

239. *Deseret News*, November 16, 1878.

240. *Labors in the Vineyard: Twelfth Book in the Faith-Promoting Series* (Salt Lake City: Juvenile Instructor Office, 1884), 65–66.

241. David Whitmer, interview with George Q. Cannon, in George Q. Cannon Journal, February 27, 1884, Historical Department Archives, Church of Jesus Christ of Latter-day Saints, Salt Lake City, UT.

242. Lucy Smith, *History of Joseph Smith by His Mother*, 147–48.

243. *Saints' Herald*, 29, March 1, 1882.

244. Joseph Smith Jr., *History of the Church of Jesus Christ of Latter-day*

Saints, ed. B. H. Roberts, 2nd ed., rev. (Salt Lake City: The Church of Jesus Christ of Latter-day Saints, 1976), 1:54–55.

245. Related by former Juvenile Court Judge C. M. Nielsen of Murray, Utah, in "Oliver Cowdery for the Defense," *Improvement Era* 46 (1943): 464.

246. David Whitmer, *An Address to All Believers in Christ* (Richmond, MO.: n.p., 1887).

247. *Millennial Star*, 40, no. 49, December 9, 1878, 772.

248. *Deseret News*, September 4, 1883.

249. *History of the Church*, 1:56.

250. *Improvement Era*, 26, no. 11, September, 1923.

251. George Godfrey, "Testimony of Martin Harris," from an unpublished manuscript copy in the possession of his daughter, Florence (Godfrey) Munson of Fielding, Utah, as quoted in Eldin Ricks, *Case of The Book of Mormon Witnesses* (Salt Lake City: Deseret News Press, 1971), 21.

252. Lucy Smith, *History of Joseph Smith by His Mother*, 148.

253. Anderson, ed. *Lucy's Book*, 455–56.

254. *History of the Church*, 1:57.

255. Ibid., 1:49.

256. *Messenger & Advocate*, 2, no. 18, March 1836, 287.

257. Jenson, *Latter-day Saints Biographical Encyclopedia*, 1:278.

258. Daniel Tyler, "Incidents of Experience," in *Scraps of Biography*, Faith-Promoting Series (Salt Lake City: n.p., 1883), 10:23.

259. *Times and Seasons*, 1, no. 1, November, 1839, 23.

260. *Journal of Discourses*, 19:38–39.

261. Wilford Woodruff, *Wilford Woodruff's Journal, 1833–1898,* ed. Scott G. Kenney (Midvale, UT: Signature Books, 1983–85), 6:508–9; spelling and punctuation were altered for readability.

262. William H. Dame, diary, manuscript, January 14, 1855, L. Tom Perry Special Collections, Harold B. Lee Library, Brigham Young University, Provo, UT.

263. Edward Stevenson, *Reminiscences of Joseph, the Prophet, and the Coming Forth of the Book of Mormon* (Salt Lake City: n.p., 1893), 14–15.

264. *Deseret Evening News*, August 16, 1878.

265. *Journal of Discourses*, 4:105–6.

266. Brigham Young, *Manuscript History*, May 5, 1867, microfilm of holograph, Church Archives.

267. Roberts, *Comprehensive History*, 1:126–27.

268. Edward Stevenson, journal, December 23, 1877.

269. *Millennial Star*, 40, no. 49, 9 December 1878, 772.

270. Joseph Smith, *The Personal Writings of Joseph Smith*, ed. Dean C. Jessee (Salt Lake City: Deseret Book, 1984), 214–15; emphasis added.

271. William Smith, "William B. Smith's Last Statement," *Zion's Ensign*, January 13, 1894, 6.

272. William Smith, "The Old Soldier's Testimony," *Saints' Herald* 31, no. 40, October 4, 1884, 643–44; emphasis added.

273. *Kansas City Journal*, June 5, 1881.

274. *Deseret News*, August 6, 1878; *Saints' Herald*, August 2, 1878.

275. *Deseret News*, November 16, 1878.

276. *Journal of Discourses*, 7:31.

277. *Personal Writings of Joseph Smith*, 214–15.

278. *History of the Church*, 1:71.

279. *Journal of Discourses*, 7:31.

280. Letter from Charles Anthon to E. D. Howe, February 17, 1834.

281. Roberts, *Comprehensive History*, 1:101.

282. "Another Gold Book Found," *Journal of Book of Mormon Studies*, 14, no. 2 (Provo, UT: FARMS, 2005: 65.

283. *Etruscan* is a term linked to the people of ancient Italy (8th–6th BC) who spoke a language termed "Etruscan" which was a non-Indo-European language. The ancient Etruscan people are believed to have no genetic link to the modern day Italians and are also believed by experts to be extinct.

284. John A. Tvedtnes, "Etruscan Gold Book from 600 BC Discovered," *Insights*, 23, no. 5 (Provo, UT: FARMS, 2003).

285. John W. Welch and Kelsey D. Lambert, "Two Ancient Roman Plates," *BYU Studies* 45, no. 2 (2006): 55–76.

286. "The Validity of the Witnesses' Testimonies," in *American Apocrypha: Essays on the Book of Mormon*, ed. Dan Vogel and Brent L. Metcalfe (Salt Lake City: Signature Books, 2002), 108.

287. Ibid., 90.

288. Ibid., 92.

289. See the entire introduction to Vogel's *Joseph Smith: The Making of a Prophet* (Salt Lake City: Signature Books, 2004).

290. "The Validity of the Witnesses' Testimonies," 93.

291. Helen Whitney, director, *The Mormons* (documentary).Frontline, 2007.

292. Robert V. Remini, "Biographical Reflections on the American Joseph Smith," in *The Worlds of Joseph Smith*, ed. John W. Welch (Provo UT: Brigham Young University Press, 2006), 23–25.

Chapter 5

293. Passages that only mention the *Urim* are Numbers 27:21; 1 Samuel 28:6. Passages which mention both the *Urim* and *Thummim* are Exodus 28:30; Levitcus 8:8; Deuteronomy 33:8; Ezra 2:63; Nehemiah 7:65.

294. See Cornelius Van Dam, *The Urim and Thummim: A Means of Revelation in Ancient Israel* (Winona Lake, IN: Eisenbrauns, 1997), 231.

295. Avraham Yaakov Finkel, *The Torah Revealed: Talmudic Masters Unveil the Secrets of the Bible* (San Francisco: Jossey-Bass), 134. See Yoma 7:3 in Jerusalem Talmud.

296. Yoma 73b, in *The Talmud of Babylonia: An American Translation*, trans. Jacob Neusner (Atlanta, GA: Scholars Press, 1984), 57.

297. Louis Ginzberg, *The Legends of the Jews* (Philadelphia: The Jewish Publication Society of America, 1946), 3:172–73.

298. See I. L. Cohen, *Urim and Thummim: The Secret of God* (Greenvale, NY: New Research, 1977), 29.

299. Ginzberg, *Legends*, 3:172.

300. Ibid., 6:69.

301. In 1999, FARMS reported that Sandia National Laboratories in New Mexico have developed radioluminescent lights that invite some interesting comparisons with the Jaredite stones. These lights

are intended to "serve needs for lighting where no electricity is readily available." Their life expectancy is about twenty years, and they are described as being "bright" and very "intense." "The radioluminescent lights are made from a highly porous silica matrix – aerogel – in which a phosphor such as zinc sulfide is dispersed. The radioactive source of the lights is tritium gas, which when incorporated into the aerogel, actually becomes chemically bonded to the aerogel matrix. The radioactivity of tritium results in beta decay. The beta particles (electrons) 'permeate through the open spaces of the aerogel and strike the phosphor particles, exciting them and causing them to emit light.' The majority of the light emitted escapes to the outside, whereas the beta radiation is contained inside the matrix. Therefore there is no appreciable external radiation. "Radioluminescent light is consistent with and supplies an intriguing parallel matching the requirements of the Jaredite stones: they are small, long-lasting, and physically harmless. It is possible that the Jaredite stones were created in a similar fashion, according to existing physical laws. Although making the molten rocks would most likely have boiled off any tritium present, it is conceivable that the Lord could have altered some other molecule in the stone to create the radioactive isotope that would produce the glowing effect. It is also possible that he could have simply infused the stones with tritium gas as the Sandia researchers have done. Interestingly, years ago President Spencer W. Kimball proposed that perhaps the Jaredite stones were illuminated 'with radium or some other substance not yet rediscovered by our scientists.' "Of course we can only speculate about the process that led to the Jaredite lights, and even the Sandia researchers are quick to caution that scientific knowledge about radio luminescent lights is still in the early stages of development. Future discoveries and further developments may more closely illuminate the manner in which the molten Jaredite stones were caused to fluoresce, but for now this latest development certainly helps us appreciate that the Book of Mormon refers to realities we are only now rediscovering" ("New Light on the Shining Stones of the Jaredites," *Pressing Forward with the Book of Mormon*, ed. John W. Welch and Melvin J. Thorne (Provo, UT: FARMS, 1999), 254–55.

302. Ludwig Koehler and Walter Baumgartner, *The Hebrew & Aramaic Lexicon of the Old Testament* (New York: E. J. Brill and Leiden, 1996), 3:1008.

303. Ginzberg, *Legends*, 1:162.

304. *Journal of Discourses* (Liverpool: Richards and Richards, 1854–86), 16:50.

305. Elias Ashmole, *Theatrum Chemicum Britannicum* (London: Grismond, 1652), sig. B; see also Deborah E. Harkness, *John Dee's Conversation with Angels: Cabala, Alchemy, and the End of Nature* (New York: Cambridge University Press, 1999), 32–33.

306. Israel Worsley, *A View of the American Indians* (New York: Arno Press, 1977), 81, 182; emphasis added.

307. Joseph Smith, *The Personal Writings of Joseph Smith*, ed. Dean C. Jessee (Salt Lake City: Deseret Book, 1984), 215.

308. Lavina F. Anderson, ed., *Lucy's Book: A Critical Edition of Lucy Mack Smith's Family Memoir* (Salt Lake City: Signature Books, 2001), 379.

309. *Tiffany's Monthly*, 5, no. 4, August 1859, 165–66.

310. *The Rod of Iron*, 1, no. 3, February 1924, 6–7.

311. Reminiscences of Joseph Knight held in the Church Archives, as cited in Milton V. Backman Jr., *Eyewitness Accounts of the Restoration* (Salt Lake City: Deseret Book, 1986), 234.

312. See Eber D. Howe, *Mormonism Unveiled* (Painesville, OH: By the author, 1834), 241–42; see also Richard Lloyd Anderson, "Joseph Smith's New York Reputation Reappraised," *BYU Studies*, 10, no. 3, (1969–1970): 296.

313. E. W. Vanderhoof, *Historical Sketches of Western New York* (Buffalo: Matthews-Northrup Works, 1907), 13–39.

314. Ellen E. Dickinson, *New Light on Mormonism* (New York: Funk and Wagnalls, 1885), 30; Hugh Nibley, *Tinkling Cymbals and Sounding Brass: The Art of Telling Tales About Joseph Smith and Brigham Young*, ed. David Whittaker (Salt Lake City: Deseret Book and FARMS, 1991), 276.

315. Carl Van Doren, ed., *Benjamin Franklin and Jonathan Edwards: Selections from their writings* (New York: Charles Scribner's Sons, 1920), 25–26.

316. Ronald W. Walker, "The Persisting Idea of American Treasure Hunting," *BYU Studies*, 24, no. 4 (Fall 1984): 235.

317. *Palmyra Reflector*, 1st ser., 2, no. 12, February 1, 1831.

318. Walker, "The Persisting Idea of American Treasure Hunting," 235.

319. Richard L. Bushman, *Joseph Smith and the Beginnings of Mormonism* (Urbana, Illinois: University of Illinois Press, 1984), 79.

320. "Joseph Smith, The Originator of Mormonism," *Chenango Union*, 30, no. 33, May 2, 1877.

321. Yvonne Chireau, "Spiritualism," in *Themes in Religion & American Culture* (Chapel Hill and London: The University of North Carolina Press, 2004), 82.

322. *Tiffany's Monthly* 5 (May 1859): 164.

323. Donna Hill, *Joseph Smith, the First Mormon* (Salt Lake City: Signature Books, 1999), 66.

324. *Tiffany's Monthly*, 5, no. 4 (August 1859): 169.

325. Richard Bushman, *Joseph Smith: Rough Stone Rolling* (New York: Alfred A. Knopf, 2005), 54, 69.

326. See P. Wilhelm Poulson, *Deseret Evening News*, August 16, 1878.

327. See letter from Oliver Cowdery to William W. Phelps, *Messenger and Advocate*, October 1834, 14.

328. "Last Testimony of Sister Emma," *Saints' Herald* 26 (1 October 1879): 289–90.

329. William Smith, interview by J. W. Peterson and W. S. Pender, 1890, Community of Christ Archives, Independence, MO.

330. Emma Smith in Edmund C. Briggs interview, Edmund C. Briggs, "A Visit to Nauvoo in 1856," *Journal of History*, January 1916, 454.

331. Letter written to the *Deseret News*, by Elder Edward Stevenson (1881).

332. David Whitmer interview with James H. Hart, 1884; as cited in Noel B. Reynolds, *Book of Mormon Authorship Revisited: The Evidence for Ancient Origins* (Provo, Utah: FARMS, 1997), 66.

333. *Address to all Believers in Christ*, a pamphlet published by David Whitmer, 1887, 12; as cited in B. H. Roberts, *A Comprehensive History of the History of the Church of Jesus Christ of Latter-day Saints* (Provo, UT: Brigham Young University Press, 1965), 1:128.

334. Dean Jessee, "Joseph Knight's Recollection of Early Mormon History," *BYU Studies*, 17, no. 1 (1976–1977): 35.

335. Royal Skousen, "Translating the Book of Mormon," in Reynolds, *Authorship Revisited*, 71–93; see also Royal Skousen, "Towards a Critical Edition of the Book of Mormon," BYU Studies, 30, no. 1 (Winter 1990).

336. Ibid.

337. Ibid.

338. Edward Stevenson, "Incidents in the Life of Martin Harris," *Millennial Star* 44 (February 6, 1882): 86–87.

339. David Whitmer's statement to Wm. H. Kelley and G. A. Blakeslee under date of September 15th, 1882; as cited in B. H. Roberts, *A Comprehensive History of The Church of Jesus Christ of Latter-day Saints* (Provo, UT: Brigham Young University Press, 1965), 1:98, 130–31.

340. Nathan Tanner Jr., reminiscence, February 17, 1909, Church of Jesus Christ of Latter-day Saints Historical Department Archives, Salt Lake City, UT.

341. *John Whitmer Historical Association Journal* 3 (1983): 51–61.

342. Harris interview with Anthony Metcalf, in Anthony Metcalf, "Ten Years Before the Mast" (n.d.,), 70–71.

343. *Kansas City Journal*, June 5, 1881.

344. Roberts, *A Comprehensive History*, 1:129.

345. "Interview with Martin Harris," *Tiffany's Monthly*, no. 6. (1856), 169–70.

346. Jessee, "Joseph Knight's Recollection of Early Mormon History," 32.

347. Joseph Smith Jr., *History of the Church of Jesus Christ of Latter-day Saints*, ed. B. H. Roberts. 2nd ed., rev. 7 (Salt Lake City: The Church of Jesus Christ of Latter-day Saints, 1976), 1:21.

348. Ibid., 1:35–36.

349. Ibid., 1:45.

350. Anderson, ed., *Lucy's Book*, 446.

351. Andrew Jenson, *Latter-day Saints Biographical Encyclopedia* (Salt Lake City: Andrew Jenson History, 1901), 1:267.

352. Anderson, ed., *Lucy's Book*, 447–49.

353. *Deseret News*, March 25, 1884.

354. *History of the Church*, 1:49.

355. Ibid., 1:53.

356. *Chenango Union*, 30, no. 33, May 3, 1877.

357. Lucy Mack Smith, *The History of Joseph Smith by His Mother* (American Fork, UT: Covenant Communications, 2000), 111.

358. Ibid., 108–109.

359. Lyndon W. Cook, ed., *David Whitmer Interviews: A Restoration Witness* (Orem, UT: Grandin Book, 1991), 150.

360. Edward Stevenson, *Reminiscences of Joseph, the Prophet, and the Coming Forth of the Book of Mormon* (Salt Lake City: n.p., 1893), 6.

361. Lorenzo Brown, "Sayings of Joseph, by Those Who Heard Him at Different Times," LDS Church Archives, Salt Lake City, UT. Emphasis added.

362. Scott G. Kenney, ed., *Wilford Woodruff's Journal* (Midvale, UT: Signature Books, 1983), 2:155–56.

363. *Times & Seasons* 3, no. 10 (March 15, 1842).

364. *History of the Church*, 5:139.

365. Ibid., 5:323–24; see also D&C 130:4–11.

366. *Journal of Discourses*, 9:87.

367. George D. Smith, ed., *An Intimate Chronicle: The Journals of William Clayton* (Salt Lake City: Signature Books in association with Smith Research Associates, 1995), 134.

368. McNamara and Maher, trans., Diez Macho, *Neophyti I* 3.465–66, as cited in Van Dam, *Urim and Thummim*, 23; emphasis added.

369. *Deseret News*, 6, 416.

Chapter 6

370. See Wilford Woodruff, *Wilford Woodruff, His Life and Labors*, comp. Matthias F. Cowley (Salt Lake City: Deseret News, 1909), 14–15.

371. Preston Nibley, *The Presidents of the Church* (Salt Lake City: Deseret Book, 1941), 50–51.

372. See B. H. Roberts, *The Life of John Taylor* (Salt Lake City: Bookcraft, 1963), 25–28.

373. B. H. Roberts, *A Comprehensive History of the Church of Jesus Christ of Latter-day Saints* (Provo, UT: Brigham Young University Press, 1965), 1:278.

374. Mark R. Grandstaff and Milton V. Backman Jr., "The Social Origins of the Kirtland Mormons," *BYU Studies*, 30, no. 2 (1990): 61.

375. Benjamin Brown, *Testimonies for the Truth* (Liverpool: S. W. Richards, 1853), as cited in George C. Lambert, "Gems for Young Folks," in *Seventeenth Book of the Faith Prompting Series* (Salt Lake City, n.p., 1915), 61.

376. Minutes of a high priest meeting in Spanish Fork, UT, February 5, 1878, Archives Division, Church Historical Department, The Church of Jesus Christ of Latter-day Saints, Salt Lake City, UT.

377. See Linda King Newell and Valeen Tippetts Avery, "Sweet Counsel and Seas of Tribulation: the Religious Life of the Women in Kirtland," *BYU Studies*, 20, no. 2 (1979–80), 156.

378. Autobiography of Jonathan Crosby, typescript, Utah State Historical Society, 5–6; see also *Woman's Exponent*, September 1, 1878, 51.

379. Ibid.

380. Andrew Jenson, *Latter-day Saints Biographical Encyclopedia* (Salt Lake City: Andrew Jenson History, 1901), 1:622.

381. Augusta Joyce Crocheron, *Representative Women of Deseret* (Salt Lake City: J. C. Graham, 1884), 24.

382. Jenson. *Latter-day Saints Biographical Encyclopedia*, 1:227.

383. Orson F. Whitney, *Life of Heber C. Kimball*, collector's ed. (Salt Lake City: Bookcraft, 1992), 15–17.

384. Ibid., 19.

385. Edward Tullidge, *The Women of Mormondom* (New York: n.p., 1877), 161–63; emphasis added.

386. Susa Young Gates, "Alexander Neibaur," *Utah Genealogical and Historical Magazine*, 9 (April, 1914): 53–63.

387. Sarah DeArmon Pea Rich (1814–1893), autobiography, typescript, Special Collections, Harold B. Lee Library, Brigham Young University, 16–18.

388. Zera Pulsipher, "History of Zera Pulsipher as Written by Himself," typescript, Special Collections, Harold B. Lee Library, Brigham Young University, 4–7.

389. *Saints' Herald*, 3 (October 1862): 79–80, 81, 82–83.

390. Joseph Young, "Autobiographical Sketch of Joseph Young," 5–6.

391. Parley P. Pratt, *Autobiography of Parley P. Pratt*, eds. Scott F. Proctor and Maurine J. Proctor (Salt Lake City: Deseret Book, 2000), 213–14.

392. Ibid., 216.

393. Ibid., 214.

Bibliography

Books

Alley, Sarah. *Account of a Trance or Vision of Sarah Alley, of Beekman Town, Dutchess County, State of New-York, Which happened on First-day Evening, the Twenty-fifth of Second Month 1798, taken from her own Mouth, the Twenty-Seventh of the same Month, in the Hearing of divers Persons*. Philadelphia: 1807.

Allwood, Philip. *A Key to the Revelation of St. John the Divine.* London: C.J.G. & F Rivington, 1829.

The Anchor Bible Dictionary. Ed. David Noel Freedman et al. 6 vols. New York: Doubleday, 1992.

Anderson, Richard L. *Investigating the Book of Mormon Witnesses.* Salt Lake City: Deseret Book, 1981.

Anderson, Lavina F., ed. *Lucy's Book: A Critical Edition of Lucy Mack Smith's Family Memoir.* Salt Lake City: Signature Books, 2001.

Angell, Truman O. "Our Pioneer Heritage." Autobiography. Special Collections, Brigham Young University, Provo, Utah.

Ashmole, Elias. *Theatrum Chemicum Britannicum*. London: J. Grismond, 1652.

Atkinson, Brooks, ed. *The Complete Essays and Other Writings of Ralph Waldo Emerson*. New York: Modern Library, 1940.

Backman, Milton V. Jr. *Eye-Witness Accounts of the Restoration*. Salt Lake City: Deseret Book, 1986.

Barlow, Nathan. *A Vision Seen By Nathan Barlow, of Freetown (Called so by the Inhabitants) Adjacent to the North End of Harlem, in the County of Kennebec, District of Maine. January 8, 1801.* Greenfield, Mass.: 1802.

Barlow, Ora Haven. *The Israel Barlow Story and Mormon Mores*. Salt Lake City, Utah: Publishers Press, 1968.

Barmby, James. *Gregory the Great*. London: Society for Promoting Christian Knowledge, 1892.

Benson, Ezra Taft. "Autobiography." *The Instructor* 80 (1945): 53–215.

Bercot, David W. *Will The Real Heretics Please Stand Up: A New Look At Today's Evangelical Church in the Light of Early Christianity*. Tyler TX: Scroll Publishing, 1999.

Bergh, Albert E. *The Writings of Thomas Jefferson*. Washington D.C.: The Thomas Jefferson Memorial Association, 1907.

Brooks, Joshua William. *A Dictionary of Writers on the Prophecies, with the Titles and Occasional Descriptions of their Works*. London: Simpkin, Marshall and Co., 1835.

Brown, Benjamin. *Testimonies for the Truth*. Liverpool: S. W. Richards, 1853.

Brown, Lorenzo. "Sayings of Joseph, by Those Who Heard Him at Different Times." Archives of The Church of Jesus Christ of Latter-day Saints, Salt Lake City, Utah

Brown, Matthew B. *The Gate of Heaven*. American Fork, Utah: Covenant Communication, 1999.

Bryant, William C., ed. *Picturesque America, or the Land We Live In*. New York: D. Appleton and Co., 1894.

Bushman, Richard L., ed. *Archive of Restoration Culture: Summer Fellows' Papers 1997–1999*. Provo Utah: Joseph Smith Fielding Institute of Latter-day Saint History, 2000.

———. *Joseph Smith and the Beginnings of Mormonism*. University of Illinois Press, 1984.

———. *Joseph Smith: Rough Stone Rolling*. New York: Alfred A. Knopf, 2005.

Callister, Tad R. *The Inevitable Apostasy, and the Promised Restoration*. Salt Lake City: Deseret Book Co., 2006.

Campbell, Alexander. *The Christian Baptist*. Cincinnati: D. S. Burnet, 1835.

———. *The Christian System: In Reference to the Union of Christians, and a Restoration of Primitive Christianity, as Plead in the Current Reformation*. Cincinnati: Standard Publishing Co., 1839.

Chamberlain, Solomon. "Short Sketch of the Life of Solomon Chamberlain, Written 11 July 1858." LDS Church Archives, Salt Lake City, Utah.

Chumney, Edward. *The Seven Festivals of the Messiah*. Shippensburg, PA: Treasure House, 1994.

Clarke, Adam. *Adam Clarke's Commentary on the Bible*. Abridged by Ralph Earle. Grand Rapids, Michigan: Baker Book House, 1967.

Classic Experiences and Adventures. Salt Lake City: Bookcraft, 1969.

Clayton, William. *An Intimate Chronicle: The Journals of William Clayton*. Editor. George D. Smith. Salt Lake City: Signature Books in association with Smith Research Associates, 1995.

Cohen, I. L. *Urim and Thummim: The Secret of God*. Greenvale, New York: New Research Publications, 1977.

Collier, Fred C. and Harwell, William S. *Kirtland Council Minute Book*. Salt Lake City, Utah: Collier's Publishing Co., 1996.

Conner, Kevin J. *Interpreting the Symbols and Types.* Portland, Oregon: City Bible Publishing, 1992.

Cowley, Matthias F. *Wilford Woodruff, His Life and Labors.* Salt Lake City: Deseret News, 1909.

Cox, Martha C. "Martha Cragun Cox (1852–1932) Autobiography, 1928–1930." Archives of The Church of Jesus Christ of Latter-day Saints, Salt Lake City, Utah.

Coy, Hannah. *A Wonderful Account of a Little Girl of nine years old, Who lives in the Town of Jericho, in the State of Vermont; by the Name of Hannah Coy.* Windsor, Vt.: 1800.

Crocheron, Augusta J. *Representative Women of Deseret.* Salt Lake City: J. C. Graham and Co., 1884.

Crosby, Jonathan. "Autobiography of Jonathan Crosby." Typescript. Utah State Historical Society.

Culver, Nathan. *Nathan Culver, A Very Remarkable Account of the Vision of Nathan Culver, late of Newton, New York: Sewing His Deistical and Vicious Principles, and How He was Converted to the Truth, by an Extraordinary and Immediate Revelation, Jan. 10, 1791.* Portsmouth, N.H.: Oracle Office, 1796.

Cuninghame, William. *A Dissertation on the Seals and Trumpets of the Apocalypse and the Prophetical Period of 1260 years.* London: Thomas Cadell, 1843.

Dahl, Larry E. and Cannon, Donald Q. *Encyclopedia of Joseph Smith's Teachings.* Salt Lake City: Bookcraft, 1997.

Dame, William H. Diary. L. Tom Perry Special Collections, Harold B. Lee Library, Brigham Young University, Provo, Utah.

Davis, Samuel. *Sermons on Important Subjects.* Boston: Lincoln and Edmands, 1810.

Dew, Sheri L. *Ezra Taft Benson: A Biography.* Salt Lake City: Deseret Book, 1987.

Dickinson, Ellen E. *New Light on Mormonism.* New York: Funk and Wagnalls, 1885.

Dowling, John. *The History of Romanism: from the Earliest Corruptions of Christianity to the Present Time.* New York: Edward Walker, 1845.

Eighth Book in the Faith-Promoting Series. Salt Lake City: Juvenile Instructor Office, 1882.

Elliot, Edward. B. *Horae Apocalypticae.* London: Seeley, Burnside, and Seeley, 1847.

Finkel, Avraham Yaakov. *The Torah Revealed: Talmudic Masters Unveil the Secrets of the Bible.* San Francisco: Jossey-Bass, 2004.

Finney, Charles G. *Memoirs of Rev. Charles G. Finney. Written by Himself.* New York: A. S. Barnes, 1876.

Firth, John F. *The Experience and Gospel Labours of the Rev. Benjamin Abbott.* Philadelphia: D&S, 1825

Four Faith Promoting Classics. Salt Lake City: Bookcraft, 1968.

Garraty, John A., ed. *Historical Viewpoints.* New York: Harper and Row, 1970.

Gaskill, Alonzo L. *The Lost Language of Symbolism.* Salt Lake City: Deseret Book, 2003.

Gates, Errett. *The Disciple of Christ.* New York: The Baker & Taylor Co., 1905.

Ginzberg, Louis. *The Legends of the Jews.* Philadelphia: The Jewish Publication Society of America, 1946.

Godfrey, George. "Testimony of Martin Harris." In possession of his daughter, Florence (Godfrey) Munson of Fielding, Utah.

Goff, Philip and Harvey, Paul, ed. *Themes in Religion & American Culture.* Chapel Hill and London: The University of North Carolina Press, 2004.

Hancock, Levi W. "Autobiography of Levi Ward Hancock, 1803–1836." Typescript. Special Collections, Harold B. Lee Library, Brigham Young University, Provo, Utah.

Harkness, Deborah E. *John Dee's Conversations with Angels: Cabala, Alchemy, and the End of Nature*. New York: Cambridge University Press, 1999.

Hibbard, Billy. *Memoirs of the Life and Travels of B. Hibbard, Minister of the Gospel*. New York: Piercy & Reed, 1843.

Hill, Donna. *Joseph Smith, the First Mormon*. Salt Lake City: Signature Books, 1999.

Hodgkin, Thomas. *Italy and Her Invaders*. Oxford: Claredon Press, 1880.

Howe, Eber D. *Mormonism Unveiled*. Painesville, Ohio: By the author, 1834.

Hughes, Richard T., ed. *The American Quest for the Primitive Church*. Champaign, Ill: University of Illinois Press, 1988.

Huntington, Oliver B. "Diary of Oliver B. Huntington, 1823–1907." Part II, Special Collections, Harold B. Lee Library, Brigham Young University, Provo, Utah.

Hyde, Orson. *Ein Ruf aus der Wüste* **(A Cry out of the Wilderness).** 1842, extract, English translation, retrieved from http://josephsmithpapers.org/paperSummary/orson-hyde-ein-ruf-aus-der-wste-a-cry-out-of-the-wilderness-1842-extract-english-translation.

Jenson, Andrew. *Latter-day Saints Biographical Encyclopedia*. Salt Lake City: Andrew Jenson History Co., 1901.

Journal of Discourses. Liverpool: F. D. and S. W. Richards, 1854–86.

Juster, Susan. *Doomsayers: Anglo-American Prophecy in the Age of Revolution*. Philadelphia: University of Pennsylvania Press, 2003.

Koehler, Ludwig and Baumgartner, Walter. *The Hebrew & Aramaic Lexicon of the Old Testament.* 3 vols. New York: E. J. Brill and Leiden, 1996.

Labors in the Vineyard: Twelfth Book in the Faith-Promoting Series. Salt Lake City: Juvenile Instructor Office, 1884.

Lambert, George C., comp. *Gems of Reminiscence, Seventeenth Book of Faith Promoting Series.* Salt Lake City: George Lambert, 1915.

Larson, A. Karl and Larson, Katharine M., eds. *Diary of Charles Lowell Walker.* 2 vols. Logan, Utah: Utah State University Press, 1980.

Launius, Roger D. and Thatcher, Linda, eds. *Differing Visions: Dissenters in Mormon History.* Urbana and Chicago, Ill: University of Illinois Press, 1994.

Luther, Martin. *Familiar Discourses.* London : Printed for W. Heptinstal, 1791.

MacGregor, Daniel. *A Marvelous Work and a Wonder; The Gospel Restored.* Reprint from the 1923 edition. Independence, Missouri: Board of Publications Church of Christ (Temple Lot), 1971.

Madsen, Truman. G. *Joseph Smith the Prophet.* Salt Lake City: Bookcraft, 1989.

Martini, Stephen A. *Radical Sects of Revolutionary New England.* Cambridge: Harvard University Press, 1982.

McConkie, Mark L. *Remembering Joseph: Personal Recollections of Those Who Knew the Prophet Joseph Smith.* Salt Lake City: Deseret Book, 2003.

Murdock, John. "Journal of John Murdock, 1792–1864." Typescript. Archive and Manuscripts, Harold B. Lee Library, Brigham Young University, Provo, Utah.

Neusner, Jacob, ed., *The Talmud of the Land of Israel.* 17 vols. The University of Chicago Press, 1988.

Nibley, Hugh. *Tinkling Cymbals and Sounding Brass: The Art of Telling Tales About Joseph Smith and Brigham Young.* Editor. David Whittaker. Salt Lake City: Deseret Book and FARMS, 1991.

Nibley, Preston. *The Presidents of the Church.* Salt Lake City: Deseret Book Company, 1941.

Nichols, James Hastings., ed. *The Mercersburg Theology.* New York: Oxford University Press, 1966.

Noble, Joseph B. "Autobiographical Sketch of Jos. Bates Noble." Mormon Biography File, Archives of The Church of Jesus Christ of Latter-day Saints, Salt Lake City, Utah.

Norton, Robert. *The Restoration of Apostles and Prophets In the Catholic Apostolic Church.* Unknown Binding: Bosworth & Harrison, 1861.

Oliver, W. H. *Prophets and Millennialists: The Uses of Biblical Prophecy in England from the 1790s to the 1840s.* Auckland: Auckland University Press, 1978.

Pastor, Ludwig. *History of the Popes, from the Close of the Middle Ages,* 40 vols. St. Louis, Mo.: B. Herder, 1898.

Pratt, Parley P. *Autobiography of Parley P. Pratt.* Eds. Scot F. Proctor and Maurine J. Proctor. Salt Lake City: Deseret Book, 2000.

Pulsipher, John. "Autobiography of John Pulsipher, 1827–1891." Special Collections, Harold B. Lee Library, Brigham Young University, Provo, Utah.

Pulsipher, Zera. "History of Zera Pulsipher as Written by Himself." Typescript. Special Collections, Harold B. Lee Library, Brigham Young University, Provo, Utah.

Reformation Bookshelf CD. 30 CDs. Still Waters Revival Books, 2003.

Reid, Robert. *The Seven Last Plagues or the Vials of the Wrath of God: a Treatise on the Prophecies in Two Parts.* Pittsburgh: D. and M. Maclean, 1828.

Remini, Robert V. *Joseph Smith*. New York: Viking Penguin, 2002.

Reynolds, Noel B., ed. *Book of Mormon Authorship Revisited: The Evidence for Ancient Origins*. Provo, Utah: FARMS, 1997.

Rich, Sarah D. P. Autobiography. Typescript. Special Collections, Harold B. Lee Library, Brigham Young University, Provo, Utah.

Richards, LeGrand. *A Marvelous Work and a Wonder*. Salt Lake City: Deseret Book, 1976.

Ricks, Eldin. *Case of The Book of Mormon Witnesses*. Salt Lake City: Deseret News Press, 1971.

Roberts, Alexander and Donaldson, James, eds. *Ante-Nicene Christian Library: Translations of the Writings of the Fathers Down to A.D. 325*. Edinburgh: T. and T. Clark, 1867.

Roberts, B. H. *A Comprehensive History of The Church of Jesus Christ of Latter-day Saints*. 6 vols. Provo, Utah: Brigham Young University Press, 1965.

———. *Life of John Taylor*. Salt Lake City: George Q. Cannon & Sons, 1892.

Robinson, Stephen E. *Are Mormons Christians?* Salt Lake City: Bookcraft, 1991.

Schauss, Hayyim. *The Jewish Festivals*. New York: Schocken Books, 1938.

Scraps of Biography, Faith-Promoting Series. Salt Lake City: Juvenile Instructor Office, 1883.

Severance, Frank H., ed. *Publications of the Buffalo Historical Society*. Buffalo, New York: Buffalo Historical Society, 1904.

Smith, Elias. *The Life, Conversion, Preaching, Travels, and Sufferings of Elias Smith*. Portsmouth, N.H.: Beck & Foster, 1816.

Smith, Joseph Fielding. *Doctrines of Salvation: Sermons and Writings of Joseph Fielding Smith*. Ed. Bruce R. McConkie. Salt Lake City: Bookcraft, 1954.

Smith, Joseph Jr. *History of The Church of Jesus Christ of Latter-day Saints*. Editor. B. H. Roberts. 2d ed., rev. 7 vols. Salt Lake City: The Church of Jesus Christ of Latter-day Saints, 1976.

———. *The Personal Writings of Joseph Smith*. Editor. Dean C. Jessee. Salt Lake City: Deseret Book, 1984.

———. *Teachings of the Prophet Joseph Smith*. comp. Joseph Fielding Smith. Salt Lake City: Deseret Book, 1976.

Smith, Lucy Mack. *The History of Joseph Smith by His Mother*. American Fork, Utah: Covenant Communications, 2000.

Smith, Uriah. *The Prophecies of Daniel and the Revelation*. Nashville: Southern Publishing Association, 1946.

Stearns, Norris. *The Religious Experience of Norris Stearns, Written by Divine Command, Shewing the Marvellous Dealings of God to His Soul, and the Miraculous Manner in which He Was Delivered from the Jaws of Death and Hell; and His Soul Set at Liberty, Likewise His Appointment to the Ministry; and Commision from on High, to Preach the Gospel to Every Creature*. Greenfield, Mass: Norris Stearns, 1815.

Stevenson, Edward. *Reminiscences of Joseph, the Prophet, and the Coming Forth of the Book of Mormon*. Salt Lake City: Stevenson, 1893.

Stone, William L. *Matthias and His Impostures: Or, the Progress of Fanaticism*. New York: Harper & Brothers, 1835.

Sullivan, Francis A. *From Apostles to Bishops: The Development of the Episcopacy in the Early Church*. New York: The Newman Press, 2001.

Taylor, John. *The Gospel Kingdom: Selections from the Writings and Discourses of John Taylor*. Editor. G. Homer Durham. Salt Lake City: Deseret Book, 1943.

Tullidge, Edward. *The Women of Mormondom*. New York: Tullidge & Crandall, 1877.

Tyndale, William and Frith, John. *The Works of the English Reformers: William Tyndale and John Frith.* Editor. Thomas Russell. London: n.p., 1831, 1:403.

Unger, Merrill. *Unger's Bible Dictionary.* Chicago: Moody Press, 1961.

Upham, Charles W. *The Life of Timothy Pickering.* Boston: Little, Brown, and Co., 1878.

Van Dam, Cornelius. *The Urim and Thummim: A Means of Revelation in Ancient Israel.* Winona Lake, Indiana: Eisenbrauns, 1997.

Van Doren, Carl, ed. *Benjamin Franklin and Jonathan Edwards: Selections from their writings.* New York: Charles Scribner's Sons, 1920.

Van Paassen, Pierre. *A Crown of Fire: The Life and Times of Girolamo Savonarola.* New York: Charles Scribner's Sons, 1960.

Vanderhoof, E. W. *Historical Sketches of Western New York.* Buffalo: Matthews-Northrup Works, 1907.

Vogel, Dan and Metcalfe, Brent L., eds. *American Apocrypha, Essays on the Book of Mormon* Salt Lake City: Signature Books, 2002.

———. *Joseph Smith: The Making of a Prophet.* Salt Lake City: Signature Books, 2004.

Ward, William. *The Fulfilment of Revelation; or Prophetic History of the Declensions and Restoration of the Christian Church.* 6 vols. London: S. M'Dowall, 1810–20.

Weisberger, Bernard A. *They Gathered at the River: The Story of the Great Revivalists and Their Impact upon Religion in America.* Chicago: Quadrangle Books, 1966.

Welch, John W. *Opening the Heavens: Accounts of Divine Manifestations 1820–1844.* Salt Lake City: Deseret Book and Provo, Utah: Brigham Young University Press, 2005.

———. *The Worlds of Joseph Smith.* Provo Utah: Brigham Young University Press, 2006.

Welch, John W. and Thorne, Melvin J. *Pressing Forward with the Book of Mormon.* Provo, Utah: FARMS, 1999.

Wesley, John. *The Works of John Wesley.* Ed., Frank Baker, et al. New York: Oxford University Press, 1975.

Whitmer, David. *An Address to All Believers in Christ.* Richmond, Mo.: 1887.

Whitney, Helen Mar. Director. *The Mormons* [Documentary]. USA: Frontline, 2007.

Whitney, Helen Mar. *A Woman's View: Helen Mar Whitney's Reminiscences of Early Church History.* Editors. Holzapfel, Jeni Broberg & Holzapfel, Richard Neitzel. Provo, Utah: Religious Studies Center, Brigham Young University, 1997.

Whitney, Orson. F. *The Life of Heber C. Kimball.* Collector's Edition. Salt Lake City: Bookcraft, 1992.

Wigger, John H. *Taking Heaven by Storm: Methodism and the Rise of Popular Christianity in America.* New York: Oxford University Press, 1998.

Willey, Chloe. *A Short Account of the Life and Remarkable View of Mrs. Chloe Willey, of Goshen, N.H.* New York: John C. Totten, 1810.

Woodruff, Wilford. *The Discourses of Wilford Woodruff.* Editor. G. Homer Durham. Salt Lake City: Bookcraft, 1946.

———. *Leaves From My Journal.* American Fork, Utah: Covenant Communications, 2005.

———. *Wilford Woodruff's Journal, 1833–1898.* Editor. Scott G. Kenney. 9 vols. Midvale, Utah: Signature Books, 1983–85.

Worsley, Israel. *A View of the American Indians.* New York: Arno Press, 1977.

Young, Brigham. *Manuscript History.* Microfilm of holograph, Archives of The Church of Jesus Christ of Latter-day Saints.

Articles

Anderson, Richard L. "Joseph Smith's New York Reputation Reappraised." *BYU Studies* 10, no. 3 (1969–70): 283–314.

Brown, Hugh B. Conference Report. October 1958.

Bushman, Richard L. "The Visionary World of Joseph Smith." *BYU Studies* 37, no. 1 (1997–98): 183–204.

Gates, Susa Young. "Alexander Neibaur." *Utah Genealogical and Historical Magazine* 9 (April, 1914): 53–63.

Grandstaff, Mark R. and Backman, Milton V. Jr. "The Social Origins of the Kirtland Mormons." *BYU Studies* 30, no. 2 (1990): 47–62.

Jessee, Dean. "Joseph Knight's Recollection of Early Mormon History." *BYU Studies* 17, no. 1 (1976): 29–39.

Kirschner, Ann. "'Tending to Edify, Astonish, and Instruct,' Published Narratives of Spiritual Dreams and Visions in the Early Republic." *Early American Studies* 1, no. 1 (Spring 2003): 198–229

Newell, Linda K. and Avery, Valeen T. "Sweet Counsel and Seas of Tribulation: the Religious Life of the Women in Kirtland." *BYU Studies* 20, no. 2 (1979–80): 151–62.

Peterson, H. Donl. "Moroni: Joseph Smith's Tutor." *Ensign*, January 1992.

Porter, Larry C. "Solomon Chamberlain-Early Missionary." *BYU Studies* 12 (Spring 1972): 314–18.

Read, Lenet H. "Joseph Smith's Receipt of the Plates and the Israelite Feast of Trumpets." *Journal of Book of Mormon Studies* 2, no. 2 (fall 1993): 110–20.

Rich, Caleb. "A Narrative of Elder Caleb Rich." *Candid Examiner* 2 (April 30–June 18, 1827): 179–97.

Skousen, Royal. "Towards a Critical Edition of the Book of Mormon." *BYU Studies* 30, no. 1 (Winter 1990): 41–69.

Tanner, Nathan Jr. Reminiscence. Archives of The Church of Jesus Christ of Latter-day Saints, Salt Lake City, Utah.

Tvedtnes, John A. "Etruscan Gold Book from 600 BC Discovered." *Insights* 23, issue. 5 (FARMS, 2003).

Wallace, Irving. "Hebrew: National Language of the U.S." *Parade Magazine*. New York: Parade Publications, May 30, 1982.

Walker, Ronald W. "The Persisting Idea of American Treasure Hunting." *BYU Studies* 24, no. 4 (Fall 1984): 429–59.

Watson, Elden J. "The 'Prognostication' of Asa Wild." *BYU Studies* 37, no. 3 (1997–98): 223–30.

Welch, John W. and Lambert, Kelsey D. "Two Ancient Roman Plates." *BYU Studies* 45, no. 2 (2006): 55–76.

Winiarski, Douglas L. "Souls Filled with Ravishing Transport: Heavenly Visions and the Radical Awakening in New England." *The William and Mary Quarterly* 61, no. 1 (January 2004): 3–46.

Wood, Gordon. "Evangelical America and Early Mormonism." *New York History* 61 (1980): 359–86.

Woodruff, Wilford. Conference Report, April 10, 1898.

Newspapers and Periodicals

Cleveland Leader.

Deseret Evening News. Salt Lake City: George Q. Cannon, 1867–1920.

Deseret News. Salt Lake City, Utah, 1865–89.

John Whitmer Historical Association Journal. Lamoni, Iowa: John Whitmer Historical Association. 1981—.

Joseph Smith, Sr. Family Reunion News. Salt Lake City: Joseph Smith, Sr. Family Reunion, 1975—

The Juvenile Instructor. Deseret Sunday School Union, 1866–1929.

Kansas City Times. Kansas City, Mo.: 1865–95.

Latter-day Saints' Messenger and Advocate. Kirtland, Ohio: F. G. Williams, 1834–37.

Latter-day Saints' Millennial Star. Manchester, England: P. P. Pratt, 1840–1937.

Palmyra Reflector. Palmyra, N.Y.: O. Dogberry, 1829–31.

The Panoplist and Missionary Magazine. Vol. 1. Boston: Farrand, Mallory and Co., 1809.

The Rod of Iron. Independence, Mo.: Zion's Religio-Literary Society. 1924–25.

Saints' Herald. Independence, Mo.: Herald House. 1860–2001.

Tiffany's Monthly. New York: Joel Tiffany, 1856–59.

Times and Seasons. Nauvoo, Illinois, 1839–46.

The Universalist Leader. Universalist Publishing House, 1925.

Wayne Sentinel. Palmyra, N.Y.: P. Tucker, 1823–53.

Woman's Exponent. Salt Lake City, 1872–1914.

Young Woman's Journal (Salt Lake City). 1889–1929.

Zion's Ensign. Independence, Mo.: Ensign Pub. Co., 1891–1932.

Illustration Sources

Lorenzo Dow. *The Life and Travels, Labors, and Writings Oof Lorenzo Dow* (New York: R. Worthington, 1881).

Elias Smith. Elias Smith, *The Life, Conversion, Travel, and Sufferings of Elias Smith*, vol. 1 (Portsmouth, N.H.: Beck & Foster, 1816).

Charles G. Finney. *Memoirs of Rev. Charles G. Finney* (New York: Fleming H. Revell Company, 1876).

John Wesley. Richard Watson, *The Life of the Rev. John Wesley* (New York: G. Lane & C. B. Tippett, 1846).

Alexander Campbell. Selina H. Campbell, *Home Life and Reminiscences of Alexander Campbell By His Wife* (St. Louis: John Burns, 1882).

John Humphrey Noyes. George W. Noyes, *Religious Experience of John Humphrey Noyes, Founder of the Oneida Community* (New York: The Macmillan Co., 1923).

Woman Seen by John the Revelator in Vision. Uriah Smith, *The Prophecies of Daniel and Revelation* (Nashville, Tennessee: Southern Publishing Association, 1946), 548.

John Calvin. Henry Stebbing, *The Life and Times of John Calvin, the Great Reformer* (New York: Robert Carter & Brothers, 1851).

Angel flying in the midst of heaven. Uriah Smith, *Daniel and Revelation* (Mountain View, California: Pacific Press Publishing Association, 1897), 632.

John Taylor. Image created by Frederick Piercy in James Linforth, *Route from Liverpool to Great Salt Lake Valley* (Liverpool: Franklin D. Richards, 1855), 75.

Lucy Mack Smith. Image created by Frederick Piercy in James Linforth, *Route from Liverpool to Great Salt Lake Valley* (Liverpool: Franklin D. Richards, 1855), 69.

Joseph Smith. Image created by Frederick Piercy in James Linforth, *Route from Liverpool to Great Salt Lake Valley* (Liverpool: Franklin D. Richards, 1855), 70.

Heber C. Kimball. Image created by Frederick Piercy in James Linforth, *Route from Liverpool to Great Salt Lake Valley* (Liverpool: Franklin D. Richards, 1855), 114.

About the Author

Trevan G. Hatch is the Ancient Scripture/Studies, World Religions & Philosophy Specialist in the Harold B. Lee Library at Brigham Young University. Trevan earned a BA in history at Brigham Young University, an MA in Jewish studies: Jewish origins at Baltimore Hebrew University/Towson University, a PhD in sociology of religion: Judaism and Islam at Louisiana State University, and is currently pursuing a master's degree in library & information science at the University of Kentucky and a doctorate in Jewish studies: Jewish origins at the Spertus Institute in Chicago. He also studied at two universities in Israel: Hebrew University of Jerusalem and the University of the Holy Land. He has taught multiple college courses at various universities relating to religion, including Early Judaism, Western Religions (Judaism, Christianity, and Islam), the Doctrine & Covenants, and Ethics. Trevan and his wife, Megan, are the parents of two girls and one boy with another on the way.

0 26575 18816 5